W9-DGD-075

The New Americans
Recent Immigration and American Society

Edited by
Steven J. Gold and Rubén G. Rumbaut

A Series from LFB Scholarly

Grassroots Coalitions and State Policy Change
Organizing for Immigrant Health Care

Margaret A. Post

LFB Scholarly Publishing LLC
El Paso 2011

Library of Congress Cataloging-in-Publication Data

Post, Margaret A.
  Grassroots coalitions and state policy change : organizing for
immigrant health care / Margaret A. Post.
    p. cm. -- (The new Americans : recent immigration and American
society)
  Includes bibliographical references and index.
  ISBN 978-1-59332-411-7 (hardcover : alk. paper)
  1. Immigrants--Medical care--Massachusetts. 2. Immigrants--Medical
care--California. 3. Health services accessibility--Massachusetts. 4.
Health services accessibility--California. 5. Pressure groups--
Massachusetts. 6. Pressure groups--California. I. Title.
  RA448.5.I44P67 2010
  362.1086'912--dc22
                                        2010039289

ISBN 978-1-59332-411-7

Printed on acid-free 250-year-life paper.

Manufactured in the United States of America.

Table of Contents

List of Tables

Preface

As I put the finishing touches on the pages of this book, immigrant rights leaders were preparing for what would be an historic rally for comprehensive immigration reform in Washington D.C. Morning news reports in the days leading up to March 21, 2010 carried voices of politicians, activists, opponents, and immigrants describing the threats of a broken immigration system and the need for its reform. Ten days before the march, President Obama met face-to-face with leaders from faith communities, labor unions, and grassroots organizations, including Ali Noorani, Executive Director of the National Immigration Forum and Chair of the Reform Immigration for America Campaign.

At the same time, the 111th Congress was narrowing in on final decisions regarding the contentious health care legislation that would be signed into law on March 23, 2010. Just hours before the passage of HR 3590 (the precursor to the landmark *Patient Protection and Affordable Care Act*), tens of thousands of immigrants and their allies convened at the National Mall. Participants demanded comprehensive reform by the end of the year, especially for the nation's estimated 12 million undocumented immigrants. Through a video broadcast, President Obama reaffirmed his commitment to the cause. Long-time supporters, including Roman Catholic Cardinal, Roger Mahony of Los Angeles, Representative Luis Gutierrez (D-IL), and Reverend Jesse Jackson, rallied the crowds to shouts of "Si Se Puede." As *The Washington Post* would report the following day, the mood that afternoon was one of hope *and* defiance.

What led to this moment in the history of immigration and health care reform? A common dynamic in these policy debates has been the growing participation of stakeholders directly affected by issues being negotiated in the halls of Congress. As the national campaigns for and against reform have unfolded, an increasingly sophisticated movement of grassroots coalitions have flexed their political muscle. This has not been a mere coincidence. Resulting from years of organization building and strategic political action, communities of color, low-income workers, immigrants, and their advocates have been an active part of these legislative battles. In the past, alliances like Reform Immigration for America and Health Care for America Now would have had only a token, if any, part in the policymaking process. Yet, within the immigration and health care debates of the last decade, organized voices demanding change have emerged from the bottom-up and demonstrated credible pressure from the outside.

2004 to 2007—the time period studied for this book—turned out to be a critical three years for the immigrant rights' movement. State and national networks grew in size and coordination, especially because of visionary leadership from experienced organizers and support from foundations dedicated to progressive social policy change. Movement leaders built on the momentum from the nation-wide immigration marches of 2006 and the hard lessons learned from a failed attempt at comprehensive reform in 2007 in order to position themselves squarely in the middle of the debate.

Likewise, this time period was essential for building momentum towards Federal health care reform. Few predicted it would reach the crescendo it has now in 2010. Yet, by 2008 at least fifteen states had proposed and/or adopted comprehensive reforms. Leading health consumer groups, labor unions, the AARP, and other non-profit organizations collaborated with policy experts and grassroots organizers in order to realize their shared goals. The election of Barack Obama catapulted both policy debates to center stage. And the ground troops were ready.

The central argument of this book is that grassroots coalitions have an integral role to play in the policymaking process. As evidenced by the stories of collective action found in the pages that follow, such coalitions are an effective tool for bridging social policy decisions with the lived experiences of everyday people. While the success of immigration reform and the viability of health care implementation remain to be seen, this study's findings indicate that with ongoing grassroots engagement in policymaking, legislative change can reflect the values and interests of groups otherwise left out of American politics.

Acknowledgements

Navigating the uncharted waters of a first book has been easier with an ocean of steadfast support. Jeffrey Prottas was an invaluable colleague from the book's inception, inviting me to collaborate on a project supported by Brandeis University's Schneider Institutes for Health Policy and the Russell Sage Foundation. Carmen Sirianni, Kelley Ready, and Marshall Ganz offered crucial perspectives that brought new clarity to the writing. Special thanks go to editors, Rubén Rumbaut and Steven Gold, and to Leo Balk.

Robert Reich, Melissa Stone, Bernie and Rollie Smith, Nan Skelton, Harry Boyte and my colleagues at the Center for Democracy and Citizenship have guided my growth as a scholar-practitioner. Ben Anderson-Nathe, Alexandra Piñeros-Shields, Lili Peaslee, and Lisa Boes helped me explore this work's intellectual and practical implications. I extend deep gratitude to Theresa Crean, Liz Steinhauser, Karla Twedt-Ball, and Zac Willette. The vibrant tapestry of my large family has made this endeavor a richer and more enjoyable journey. I am indebted to my siblings and to my parents—James and Jeannette Post—my models of leadership in public life.

This work would not have been possible without the contributions of the many individuals I interviewed. My hope is that their experiences and vision of better health care for all people are reflected accurately. Any factual or interpretive mistake that may have been made is my own.

I have written this book in honor of the women of the Jane Addams School for Democracy, who taught me the meaning of citizenship, and in memory of my life's anchor, Claudia Sophia Post, 1921-2005.

Waltham, Massachusetts, April 2010

CHAPTER ONE

Introduction

Policymaking in American government presents significant barriers to those on the margins of political life. Legal status, a lack of education and economic power, social and racial disparities are but a few factors that restrict active participation in the democratic process. For the foreign-born, each wave of immigration has been marked with rises and falls in access to power and public influence. Today, we stand at one such historic crossroads in the United States.

Comprehensive immigration reform has been a consistent dimension of current national policy debates, with the realities of undocumented immigration at the center. Estimates from the U.S. Census, the Department of Homeland Security, and the Pew Hispanic Center confirm that the most recent wave of unauthorized migration was one of the largest and most rapidly growing in the past century (Hoefer, Rytina, and Baker 2009; Passel and Cohn 2009). Pro and con, the 2008 presidential candidates sounded the drumbeat: something must change to protect our borders; newcomers without status should be treated humanely, but with justice; we have to confront the flows of undocumented immigration.

Since the mid-1990s, there has been a trend in local, state, and federal policy that aims to limit social supports and educational resources for legally-residing, foreign-born adults and children. The passage of the *USA Patriot Act* in 2001 fueled an anti-immigrant trend in social policymaking. Inconsistencies in increased enforcement and control by the U.S. Citizenship and Immigration Services, along with local ordinances that target undocumented workers have threatened civil liberties and, in many cases, have catalyzed explicit intimidation of foreign-born residents, regardless of status. Such cases have been documented, primarily at the grassroots level and among community-based organizations that work with immigrant families. These changes in public policy and practice have heightened fear and anxiety among all immigrants and their service providers. Together, this reality paints a bleak picture for immigrant wellbeing in the United States.

Simultaneous to this trend in American public policy, the nation has witnessed a changing landscape in health policy. As individual states moved forward on legislative reform, a renewed public debate emerged about how to address the high rates of the uninsured and the problems of unequal access to care. Beginning with Massachusetts' historic reform in 2006 that required all residents to have health insurance, national attention turned to how state policy change and implementation could address issues of access, affordability, and quality of care. In March 2008, the Kaiser Commission on Medicaid and the Uninsured released profiles of those states that were proceeding with comprehensive health care reforms (Kaiser 2008). Maine, Massachusetts, and Vermont had enacted some form of universal coverage and an additional twelve states were exploring policy options for systematic health reform that could increase access to coverage for the uninsured. A resolute commitment to health reform came with the election of Barack Obama, and, at this writing, the *Patient Protection and Affordable Care Act* and the accompanying *Health Care and Education Reconciliation Act* of 2010 were on their way to final votes in Congress. In both policy arenas, state and federal lawmakers have considered policy alternatives that include coverage for legal permanent residents and the undocumented.

At a time when it seems unlikely to garner support for progressive public policies, especially those that benefit the foreign-born, health reform initiatives in Massachusetts and California demonstrate how two ostensibly contradictory policy realities existed together. The cases of immigrant health policy change in these states—and the stories of the immigrant-based organizations involved in trying to change them—are a microcosm of this contemporary phenomenon. Policy change between 2004 and 2007 was an auspicious occasion to examine how grassroots coalitions advanced a policy agenda based on values of access, affordability, and quality. It was also an opportunity to examine how the interests of a traditionally marginal group were embedded within a larger strategy for policy change. These policy events and the circumstances of coalition building surrounding them provided the basis for this study of how and why grassroots alliances incorporated immigrant health interests in their policy agenda, and what organizational processes facilitated or inhibited their effectiveness and success.

OVERVIEW
This study investigates how statewide coalitions facilitated the incorporation of immigrant interests in state health

policy change. Its primary objective was to understand coalitions as instruments of policy change through a focus on statewide coalitions that included access to care for immigrants in their organizing goals. The cases of Massachusetts and California between 2004 and 2007 tell a story of how immigrant health coverage was a part of health policy reforms for which these statewide coalitions advocated. Policy outcomes varied during this time, yet these were hard won successes that required much effort to insert immigrant care into legislative proposals and to lobby for its inclusion.

As a mediating structure, coalitions are one vehicle by which immigrant-based organizations can access the policymaking environment and have influence on policy decisions that directly affect the lives of their constituents and clients. The pages that follow examine the role of community-based groups as intermediaries, organizing around the social policy interests of immigrants. In Massachusetts and California, policy advocates and community organizers formed coalitions that would advance the health priorities of access and affordability. Within this context, certain organizational factors impacted how immigrant health interests were and were not protected in the process. These included coalition formation, strategies and tactics for integrating immigrant coverage into new state health policy, and the extent to which they achieved success. The analysis of coalitions illustrates how they were used to promote immigrant interests in an uncertain policy arena, and how these types of coalitions can provide voice and power for incorporating immigrant interests in the policymaking process. This focus on organizational development, growth, and capacity building complements a focus on policy change, in that internal organizational outcomes are integrated with external policy outcomes as elements of success.

The findings indicate that, especially for marginalized groups, coalition building can be an effective strategy for the inclusion of interests in policy change. For immigrant political gains to be made at the state level, one effective intermediary mechanism is coalitions of mixed organizational type that promote immigrant interests in relationship to the health interests of other groups. While the coalitions studied used similar organizing strategies, they made variable policy gains. Certain organizational factors influenced the incorporation of immigrant health interests based on three outcomes: inter-organizational partnerships, internal organizational capacity building, and claims-making in the policy arena. Inter-organizational partnerships and internal capacity development were found to make a difference in successfully incorporating immigrant interests through the statewide health coalitions, even with variable policy change success. The theoretical framework developed from the findings explains how this type of intermediary group can facilitate the incorporation of immigrant interests within broader political arenas.

IMPLICATIONS
Mediating institutions are positioned between governments and the polity (Skocpol and Fiorina 1999; Wolbrecht 2005). They can bridge the political interests and needs of the people with the goals, priorities, and laws of the State. As a vehicle for democratic inclusion, mediating institutions are central to the vibrant traditions of civic participation in the United States (Wolbrect 2005).

Grassroots activism in this regard has enabled the citizenry to have a voice in policymaking (Sirianni 2009). Through legislative advocacy and lobbying, protests and rallies, and other forms of civic leadership, mediating institutions have provided pathways by which ordinary people have participated in processes of public decision-making (Boyte and Kari 1996; Gecan 2002; De Souza Briggs 2008). Especially for the poor and working class, racial and ethnic minorities, and women, mediating institutions, such as civic associations, faith-based, voluntary groups and labor unions, have been a source for increasing influence and political power in the public arena (Skocpol 2003).

The rise in the share of U.S. foreign-born residents over the last twenty years has brought issues of immigrant incorporation to the forefront for governments, social service agencies, and the communities into which newcomers settle (Ku and Papademetriou 2007; Schmidley 2001). Social, economic, and political conditions play a significant role in adaptation as new immigrants settle in urban and increasingly more suburban communities (Carnegie 2003; DeSipio 2000; Fix 2002; Portes and Rumbaut 2001). Economic uncertainty and a lack of adequate access to education, housing, health care and social services foster an environment of instability for immigrants. These factors shape the context in which immigrants seek to develop political efficacy and influence, and have catalyzed public action for policy change among organizations that support newcomers.

Anti-immigrant sentiment is not a new phenomenon in the history of U.S. immigration, nor is the struggle of marginal groups to have a voice in the political process. In many respects, what we witness today is a vestige of the past. Pervasive anti-immigrant sentiment, racial and ethnic tension, and the overall decrease in access to public benefits, have stimulated an increased acquisition of English language skills and U.S. citizenship (Fix, Passel, and Sucher 2003; Gerstle and Mollenkopf 2001; Gilbertson and Singer 2003). Grassroots' voter engagement initiatives among new citizens have become more prevalent. The national debates about federal immigration reform and the outrage at large-scale immigration raids have sparked widespread activism throughout the country, marked in particular by the rallies held in the Spring of 2006 (Wang and Winn 2006; Capps et al. 2007).

To improve the wellbeing of immigrant children and families many community-based organizations have had to engage in organizing and advocacy campaigns for policy change. In response to state policies targeting a reduction in services, national immigrant rights groups, community-based ethnic coalitions, and service providers have mobilized to advocate for policies that meet the basic needs of the U.S. immigrant population (McGarvey 2004; Applied Research Center 2002). Such efforts have the potential for increased political pressure and influence on policy outcomes, especially in cities and states where there is a growing naturalized electorate. It is at state and municipal levels of government where some of the most compelling evidence exists for how the current wave of newcomers is becoming a force within American political and civic life. Policy and electoral events within this context, and the collective action that has accompanied them, indicate a broader role for community and advocacy organizations in influencing policymaking and practice that affect immigrant communities.

Where a growing literature points to the role of community-based organizations in immigrant political integration (Ramakrishnan and Bloemraad 2008), there is limited research about how institutional actors build capacity for public influence, impact policy, and, thereby, support immigrant civic and political development (Però and Solomos 2010). More empirical work is needed to understand the organizational processes that catalyze such actions and lead to successful outcomes. As the share of the foreign-born grows in the United States and the number of naturalized citizens increases, it is critical that we develop a deeper understanding about what institutional arrangements and organizational structures facilitate this dimension of political incorporation. This book begins to fill the gap by investigating how health policy coalitions incorporated immigrant interests in their organizing strategies for policy change. Its central premise is that statewide policy coalitions are one necessary and effective organizational mechanism by which immigrant interests are incorporated into the policymaking process.

Therefore, the research study has implications for both theory and practice. First, a theory about the role of coalitions as mediating institutions in immigrant political incorporation is developed using exploratory case methods. This objective aims at improving the analytic tools used to investigate the relationships between organizational factors and the incorporation of immigrant interests in policy change. The findings provide the foundation from which future research can test hypotheses developed here. Second, the research illuminates best practices for immigrant-based, community organizations interested in strengthening and expanding their capacity for public policy change and political action. By examining these organizations within coalitions of mix-organizational type, noteworthy practical knowledge was uncovered for use by community organizers and advocates who seek to develop a strategy for policy change.

Chapters Two and Three provide a multi-disciplinary discussion of what is known about immigrant politicization and the role of community-based organizations in that process. Chapter Two integrates the sociological literature about the adaptive experiences of immigrants and new citizens with scholarship from political science about the structures and institutions that facilitate or inhibit involvement in political processes. It also draws on new scholarship about the organizing capacity and activism of immigrant organizations, and makes use of findings from research conducted by policy institutes and program evaluations implemented by foundations with their grantees. Where little research in this area has been done before, these scholars capture key characteristics of contemporary immigrant organizations that support the findings from this study. This discussion provides an initial framework of how the integration of immigrant interests is a dimension of political incorporation, building on what Andersen and Cohen (2005) describe as the "incorporative" behavior of organizational actors (187). Chapter Three explains how the study's initial propositions were formulated into an overarching theoretical framework that emerged in the analysis of organizational processes and campaign outcomes. The methodology used to develop this theory is explained in Chapter Four.

The case narratives and analysis are presented in Chapters Five and Six, and are based on three conceptual ideas: inter-organizational partnerships, internal capacity building, and claims-making success. The accounts of immigrant health policy change that occurred in Massachusetts and California from 2004-2007 have a particular focus on the participation of immigrant organizations in that process. Following the narratives and using the three outcomes common in both states, Chapter Six explains why the coalitions worked in some ways—and not in others—to integrate immigrant interests in the policymaking arena. In addition to an analysis of organizational conditions, this chapter includes a discussion of how and why the operating environment influenced organizational and policy outcomes. The concluding chapter explores the implications of the findings for both theory and practice, and emphasizes the challenges of coalition building and access to care for the undocumented.

CHAPTER TWO

Organizational Pathways to Political Incorporation: The Role of Coalitions

OVERVIEW

Much of the scholarship on the immigrant experience focuses on factors that influence how individuals and groups adapt to host communities. Another approach that has received less scholarly attention examines how community-based organizations and grassroots advocacy groups engage in civic and political activities that help immigrants meet their basic needs. Though much has been learned about the individual process of political engagement, a number of organizational avenues to political power building remain unexplored. In order to fully understand contemporary pathways of immigrant political incorporation, we need to examine how coalitions of community- and immigrant-based organizations advance immigrant policy interests.

PATHWAYS TO POLITICAL INCORPORATION

Scholarship on the adaptive experience of immigrants[1] provides a valuable foundation for understanding the social, economic, and cultural forces that affect one's ability to participate in the political life of a host community.[2] This includes extensive research on rates of naturalization and the correlating socio-economic factors, voting behavior, positions held in public office, and the extent to which the interests of particular ethnic groups are incorporated into policy (Bass and Casper 1999; Ramakrishnan 2005; Ramakrishnan and Espenshade 2001; Skerry 1993; DeSipio, Masuoka, and Stout 2006). While models of assimilation and acculturation[3] tend to explain individual level determinants of engagement (such as age, education, and socioeconomic status), they rarely account for the organizational processes that facilitate civic and political involvement. Much of this literature focuses on immigrants' individual or group experiences, without closely examining how organizations and institutional arrangements may also impact outcomes of involvement (Ramakrishnan and Bloemraad 2008; Wong 2006; Lee, Ramakrishnan, and Ramírez 2006).

---

[1] For the purposes of this discussion, the term "immigrants" includes foreign-born residents of all statuses, recognizing that there is great diversity among this population. For example, the type of status held by a newcomer, including as a legal permanent resident, refugee, asylee, or unauthorized migrant, will likely impact his or her experience of settlement and adaptation.

[2] See Portes and Rumbaut (2006) and Waters and Ueda (2007).

[3] See essential work on segmented assimilation, including Portes and Zhou (1993), Portes and Rumbaut (2001), and Zhou (1997).

Incorporation into American civic and political life can begin during the early years of residence among first generation immigrants, accounting for country of origin and host country reception (Bueker 2006; Portes and Rumbaut 2006). Activities in local institutions — schools and churches, ethnic organizations, labor unions, and other local non-profits — also orient newcomers to the patterns of participation and involvement in their new homes (DeSipio 2000; Portes and Rumbaut 2006; Wong 2006). For example, when immigrants come together in response to community problems, they build community with one another, enhance their civic skills, and develop networks across ethnic groups that form a base of power for future public action. With these capacities, immigrants are better equipped to respond to issues of concern, including outbreaks of neighborhood violence, incidents with the police, problems with local schools or service agencies, and access to adequate health care, housing, employment, and child care (DeSipio 2000; Portes and Rumbaut 2006). It is these experiences that can drive eligible immigrants to seek naturalization, and in some cases, go on to positions of civic and political leadership (Gilbertson and Singer 2003).

Generally, research on patterns of citizenship, voting behavior, and political party involvement has found that these modes of participation are connected to levels of education, income, and length of residence among immigrants.[4] One's experience of migration, settlement and host country reception, and his or her transnational ties to the home country have been found to affect political

---

[4]For examples, see DeSipio (2000, 2001, 2002); Diaz (1996); Portes and Rumbaut (2001), Ramakrishnan (2005).

participation, primarily in terms of citizenship acquisition (Bueker 2006; Portes, Escobar, and Arana 2008; Ramakrishnan 2005; and Bass and Casper 1999). For example, Bass and Casper (1999) conclude that citizenship acquisition and registering to vote are first steps in the process of becoming politically engaged. They find that naturalized immigrants who are more economically and socially established are more likely to register to vote and participate in elections. They, along with DeSipio (2001, 2002) also find that longer length of residence, homeownership, more education, and higher incomes are all indicators of political adaptation. Portes and Rumbaut (2006) further emphasize the necessary role of naturalization in an immigrant's adaptive experience (140). However, Wong (2006) suggests that naturalization may not be the only motivating step towards political involvement. She argues that other types of engagement activities should be examined more closely, especially those found within community organizations.

Individual and group-level factors undoubtedly make a contribution to a newcomer's increased interest in and capacity for civic and political engagement. This analysis complements the landmark work of Verba, Schlozman, and Brady (1995) who point to access, motivation, and resources as the dominant factors in an individual's engagement. The findings in the immigrant political participation literature are consistent with those in the general population: voting has declined overall among all members of the polity; active political participation has strong positive correlations with levels of education and income; and greater access to economic, political, and social capital increase the likelihood of participation in the electoral and policymaking process. However, the political socialization process for new immigrants is shaped by unique social, economic, cultural, and institutional barriers not necessarily faced by members of the general population (Bloemraad 2006; Portes and Rumbaut 2006). Moreover, organizations rooted in immigrant communities have a critical role to play in breaking down these barriers to engagement (Wong 2006).

Despite common public discourse, immigrants face different challenges today than during the last great wave of immigration at the turn of century (DeSipio 2001; Gerstel and Mollenkopf 2001; Jones-Correa 2005; Wolbrecht 2005).[5] Access to the formal political arena for both the native and foreign born alike has become increasingly limited to those with economic stability, language and literacy skills, and education (DeSipio 2001; Schlozman, Verba and Brady 1999). It is well-documented that social and economic barriers to adaptation and mobility are different, and some would argue, more extreme, for immigrants today than for their European counterparts of the early 20th century (Jones Correa 2005; Portes and Zhou 1993; Portes and Rumbaut 2001). In particular, the changing structure of the U.S. economy and a decline in labor market mobility make it less likely that new immigrants are able to establish economic stability within the first and second generations (Portes and Rumbaut 2001; Kaushal, Reimers and Reimers 2007). Racial discrimination and concentrated poverty in the

---

[5] See Portes and Rumbaut (2006) and Chapter Three of Portes and Rumbaut (2001) for discussion of factors that influence contemporary assimilation. In their theoretical framing and analysis, the authors emphasize the heterogeneous nature of both the immigrant experience and the receiving communities.

urban core are also barriers to social and economic mobility. Substantial gaps exist in educational attainment outcomes among ethnic groups and between generations (Suárez-Orozco and Suárez-Orozco 2001; 2007; Portes and Rumbaut 2001; and Zhou 1997). These challenges impact opportunities for political engagement and influence. Cultural norms and processes of political participation that have discouraged the involvement of the poor, uneducated electorate exacerbate these challenges further for newcomers.

Bloemraad (2006) suggests that the organizations and institutions in which immigrants participate shape factors of adaptation and it is the *interactive process* between individuals, communities, organizations, and governments that is so central to the immigrants' political experience. Until recently, most literature on political incorporation focused on an individual's resources, skills, and interests, not an investigation of contextual or societal-level factors (Bloemraad 2006, 7). Bloemraad argues that, "the major weakness of the behavioral tradition is its inattention to institutional contexts," and that the individual or group perspective alone limits a more complete understanding of the process by which newcomers incorporate politically (7-9). Without analyzing the institutional arrangements through which immigrants politically incorporate, we cannot fully explain how they integrate as members of American democratic society (Bloemraad 2006; Andersen and Cohen 2005; Wong 2006). If we better understand how organizations mediate barriers and influence pathways to engagement, we can begin to understand how contemporary immigrants and their interests are brought to bear on American political life (Andersen and Cohen 2005).

Ramakrishnan and Bloemraad's (2008) edited volume contributes significantly in this regard, and holds particular salience when considering how immigrant interests are translated into goals for viable political action through organizational activity. Integrating perspectives from sociology, political science, and ethnic studies, the authors account for the role of organizations as facilitators of engagement, making the case that organizations are critical links in the process of immigrant integration. They argue that organizational dimensions of political incorporation are largely unexplored and require theoretical models that go beyond a solely individual or group-based analysis. Ramakrishan and Bloemraad see the lack of attention paid to organizations as problematic for understanding the multi-dimensionality of contemporary trends in civic and political engagement. They frame this lack of research in the following way:

> The present-day debate in the immigrant adaptation literature is largely silent on the role of civic and political participation or the formation of community organizations. We lack a clear understanding of the factors that catapult some organizations and groups to political prominence and leave others at the periphery of local influence, nor do we fully understand the role of state actors and mainstream social institutions in allocating and shaping power and access to political resources (7).

Però and Solomos (2010) echo this theme, noting that it is necessary to examine broader and deeper factors of the process of incorporation, especially the organizational contexts and forms of political mobilization through self-help organizations and community networks (2, 10).

MEDIATING INSTITUTIONS & POLITICAL INCORPORATION

Mediating institutions are critical to the inclusion of disadvantaged groups in American democracy. According to Wolbrecht (2005), mediating institutions include social movements, political parties, and interest organizations that serve as "agents of political mobilization and socialization," (103). These institutions play a specific role in educating and mobilizing the citizenry for political engagement, and have the capacity to facilitate and inhibit participation and representation in policymaking and governance (103-104). However, like immigrant adaptation, the nature of these institutions and their relationship to immigrant political interests is different today than in the past (Wolbrect 2005).

Historically, organizations of immigrant political incorporation like labor unions, political parties, urban political machines, and churches once played a significant role in the process of immigration mobilization and socialization: guiding them through the naturalization process, mobilizing them for elections, and engaging them in collective action (Andersen and Cohen 2005; Gerstle and Mollenkopf 2001; DeSipio 2000, Wong 2006). Immigrants prepared for deeper participation in public life through mediating institutions: they acquired literacy and employment skills, learned about American government, and were exposed to cultural norms and values of democratic engagement. Depending on the capacity of such local institutions, immigrants could also contest for power, often making important political gains for marginalized groups. Even amidst the corruption that could saturated political party machines, these types of mediating institutions served a necessary role in the integration of immigrant interests within the public arena (Andersen and Cohen 2005; Soyer 2006).

At the turn of the 20th century, community institutions acted as a mechanism through which immigrants engaged in American public life (Sterne 2001).[6] Settlement houses, ethnic associations, neighborhood networks, churches, and synagogues were indirect entrées into the political arena for people who would otherwise have been excluded, especially because of limited language skills, a lack of citizenship, or unemployment (Boyte and Kari 1996; Koerin 2003). They were not only places where newcomers went for social supports. Within this context, immigrants also became aware of and discussed the problems and possibilities of life in the United States (Sterne 2001). From these forums some immigrants stepped into formal public roles, positioning themselves among the political elites. They established credibility by running for local office, making specific demands on local government, and winning political gains on behalf of their interests and those of their community (Sterne 2001; Portes and Rumbaut 2006).

Over a century later, immigrant service providers, community and neighborhood groups,[7] unions, and

---

[6] Also see Wong (2006); Portes and Rumbaut (2006); and Bloemraad (2006).

[7] Diaz (1996) and DeSipio (2002) have both found that strong relationships exist between immigrant political participation and membership in civic associations. Diaz (1996) advocates that because organizational membership has a strong impact on the political participation of Puerto Ricans and Mexican Americans, greater efforts should be made to support nonprofit and

advocacy organizations, especially at the local level, continue to be situated as connectors between new immigrant communities and government (Applied Research Center 2002; Carnegie 2003; McGarvey 2004; Wolbrecht 2005). Religious institutions, social services, health clinics, and neighborhood and ethnic associations are a bridge between immigrants and U.S. culture and society (Andersen and Cohen 2005; Wong 2006; Portes and Rumbaut 2006, 2001; DeSipio 2001). They meet basic needs, providing food, housing, health care, language instruction, employment services and other supports that aid immigrants in their transition. These community-based organizations also create the social and cultural contexts in which immigrants come to understand themselves as members of American society.

While the vast majority of such groups are focused on service provision, some organizations have moved beyond this model, rekindling the roots of traditional mediating institutions and aiming to empower immigrants for active participation in democratic life. In addition to meeting the social service needs of a local immigrant community, these organizations may also provide naturalization services and voter education, lobby for policy change and improved access to benefits for immigrants, or organize political action on behalf of their constituents' interests (Wong 2006; De Graauw 2008). Advocacy groups, ethnic associations, and immigrant rights organizations help to break down barriers to political participation for new immigrants and

---

grassroots organizations focused on Latino political empowerment. He posits that membership itself is one important avenue for increasing the political participation of Latinos.

facilitate broader involvement in a variety of civic activities (Applied Research Center 2002; McGarvey 2004; Wong 2006; De Graauw 2008). These contemporary forms of mediating institutions bring into the public domain the interests and rights of immigrants—many of whom do not have formal membership as citizens (Andersen and Cohen 2005; Bloemraad 2006; Jones-Correa 2005; Wong 2006; De Graauw 2008). Staff and advocates from these organizations also can buffer the unwelcoming context of reception that immigrants may experience in state and local public agencies, often serving as language and cultural translators within schools, immigration offices, and social welfare agencies (DeSipio 2001; Blomenraad 2006).[8]

Accessibility to ethnic- and community-based organizations is particularly relevant to the development of immigrant political power, recognizing that these institutions function as intermediaries in the process of incorporation. Because new immigrants and refugees not only settle in traditional gateway cities, but also in smaller, more homogenous communities, the density of organizations that support them varies from state to state and within metropolitan areas (Wong 2006; Singer 2004; Singer 2008; Logan 2007). Where there is a greater concentration of immigrants, it is more likely that a community will have developed extensive networks of mutual assistance associations (MAA), ethnic-based service providers, community development groups, and immigrant rights organizations (Applied Research Center

---

[8] See also Portes and Rumbaut (2001) for how contextual factors such as government policies, host community's reception, and immigrant social networks impact adaptation.

2002). As immigrant groups become more established in a given area, they develop strong networks of support and influence within these organizations and in the wider community (DeSipio 2000; Portes and Rumbaut 2006; Menjivar 2000). The composition of this organizational infrastructure in a given community will affect an immigrant groups' ability to respond to political opportunities and threats, and to leverage support for its interests. The influence of diverse groups expands as the growth of new immigrant communities transforms gateway metropolitan areas (Logan 2007; Singer 2004). This has been seen not only in larger cities like Boston, Chicago, Los Angeles, and New York with vibrant traditions of hosting newcomers, but also in newer gateway cities that, in some cases, are small towns and cities with little racial and ethnic diversity.

It is evident that new organizational forms are taking the place of intermediary mechanisms that have weakened over time (Wong 2006; Andersen and Cohen 2005; McGarvey 2004). These ethnic- and community-based organizations have replaced older versions of mediating institutions, such as political parties (Baum and Shipilov 2006). Andersen and Cohen (2005) see a direct connection between organizational activity and immigrant political incorporation, affirming that many of the newer mediating institutions play increasingly important political roles as they facilitate more "points of entry" to express and act on their political interests and demands (200). The work of the Applied Research Center (2002),[9] McGarvey (2004),

---

[9] In *Mapping the Immigrant Infrastructure*, the Applied Research Center (2002) explains four types of immigrant and refugee organizations that "ease the barriers to immigrants' transition

Ramakrishnan and Viramontes (2006), and Wong (2006) suggests an organizational typology that is useful for explaining the political nature of immigrant organizations. A central theme among these scholars is that organizations of varying types promote and engage in a range of political activity. Some focus on individual modes of participation like naturalization and voter engagement while others focus on collective strategies such as direct-action campaigns and policy change initiatives. Together, this work points to the ways in which specific types of immigrant-based organizations have improved their skills for public action, and in turn, increased their capacity as vehicles of political incorporation.

Table 1 provides an overview of these types of organizations, and summarizes the nature of activity generally found within each type. "Public action" encompasses both civic and political activities that contribute to an organization's overall capacity for public engagement in political processes. This framing builds on Ramakrishnan and Bloemraad's (2008) distinction between civic and political engagement that reflects an important analytic advancement in the literature and goes beyond citizenship and electoral participation as the primary measures of political activity and indicators of incorporation.

---

from their home countries to U.S. Society" (4). These include 1) mutual assistance associations and ethnically-based service providers; 2) community organizing groups; 3) immigrant rights organizations; and 4) cross-over organizations (defined as a "new breed of organization" that meets specific needs of an immigrant community not addressed by other groups) (12).

TABLE 1: Immigrant-Based Organizations & Public Action[10]	
Type	**Nature of Public Action**
• Mutual Assistance Associations • Ethnic-based Service Providers	• Non-profit, service providers *Little to no capacity for public action*
• Ethnic Civic Associations[11]	• Leadership development • Grassroots mobilization • Local advocacy and civic engagement • Some labor organizing *Local capacity for public action*
• Immigrant Rights Organizations	• Policy advocacy • Grassroots mobilization • Coalition building *Local, state, and limited national capacity for public action*
• Community Organizing Groups • Worker Centers	• Multi-issue, multi-racial direct action • Leadership development • Some coalition building *Local capacity for public action; Limited capacity for state public action.*
• Labor Unions	• Unionization of low-wage workers • *Recent support for immigrant workers* • Some policy advocacy on immigrant-related issues * *Local, state and national capacity for public action*

---

[10] Adapted from Applied Research Center (2002), McGarvey (2004), Andersen and Cohen (2005), and Ramakrishnan and Vigamontes (2006). Summary also expands Wong's (2006) organizational groupings (98).

[11] Includes "Cross-over organizations" that meet immigrant interests as defined by the Applied Research Center (2002).

CLAIMS-MAKING & POLITICAL INCORPORATION

Whether or not groups successfully make demands in the public arena and have influence over government decisions are important benchmarks of democratic inclusion (Wolbrecht 2005). Impacting elections and holding public office are two such dimensions of claims-making power. Generations of new immigrants have had powerful influences on elections as well as on government action through interest group pressure (Tichenor 2002). The increasing naturalization rates among the foreign born along with their participation in local, state, and national elections indicate the potential electoral power of new immigrant groups, especially Latinos and Asian Americans (Jones-Correa 2005; Ramakrishnan 2005; DeSipio 2001). Ramakrishan (2005) cautions, however, that while there has been sizable growth among the first- and second-generation electorate since 1970, the magnitude of this growth and its potential impact has been overestimated (27). First and second generation immigrants have also leveraged positional power through municipal and statewide elections and through organizational leadership in the business and non-profit sectors (Ramakrishnan and Vigamonte 2006; Carnegie 2003; Bloemraad 2006). Even as the number of naturalized citizens, immigrant community leaders, and elected officials who are immigrant or of recent immigrant-descent grows, influencing political outcomes also depends on the ability to mobilize support for group interests and leverage change on their behalf.

To what extent do mediating institutions exist today that can enable the successful incorporation of immigrant political interests in the public arena? With the changing shape of American civic culture,[12] the declining role of civic associations,[13] and the overall weakening of U.S. political parties, this question is of central importance to scholars of immigrant political incorporation (Gerstle and Mollenkopf 2001; Ramakrishnan and Bloemraad 2008; Wong 2006). The emergence of scholarship documenting the decline of civic associations in the United States raises questions as to whether such associations are available to today's immigrants as they had been in the past.[14] Where participation in the electoral arena is often restricted to those who have become U.S. citizens, have college or advanced degrees, and stable incomes (DeSipio 2000; Hardy-Fanta 1993; Portes and Rumbaut 2006, 2001; Ramakrishnan 2005), political opportunities do exist through local institutions for those who would otherwise not have access to making demands in the public arena. School reform initiatives, faith-based and neighborhood activism, campaigns by labor unions and worker centers, and issue-based advocacy have been forums for the civic and political engagement of many immigrants (Andersen and Cohen 2005; Applied Research Center 2002; Flores 1997; McGavery 2004; Ramakrishnan and Viramontes 2006; Wong 2006).

By and large, community organizations that catalyze civic and political initiatives have varying degrees of

---

[12] See Sirianni and Friedland (2001).

[13] See Skocpol and Fiorina (1999) and Skocpol (2003) for discussion of declining role of civic associations and the implications for 21st century American society.

[14] Most notable among these, is Robert Putnam's, *Bowling Alone* (2001). See also Skocpol (2003) and Sirianni and Friedland (2001) for discussion of limitations to Putnam's thesis.

success: they confront powerful anti-immigrant interests, tend to lack adequate staff resources and funding support, and can be marginalized in the public arena by other, more powerful, interest groups. That said, the active engagement of newcomers in collective problem solving strategies has been documented as central to their integration into democratic life in the United States (McGarvey 2004, 15). Building on Verba, Schlozman and Brady's (1995) work, McGarvey (2004) suggests that *engagement* is different from service delivery and advocacy, and that network building, empowerment, and leadership development are central to effective civic participation strategies (15). Even if a group's ultimate goals are not achieved, organization building and civic learning can occur. These conclusions are supported by Wong's (2006) study that examines how current civic institutions mobilize immigrants. She challenges the assumption that immigrants' "failure" to actively participate in politics is rooted in individual shortcomings, limitations, or personal attitudes. Rather, she finds that "in the absence of a strong party presence at the local level, community organizations are among the only civic institutions mobilizing immigrants in their local communities," (201). Both McGarvey and Wong reinforce the centrality of intermediary groups and community institutions in the pathway to immigrant political incorporation.

These conclusions, along with those made by Ramakrishnan and Bloemraad (2008), lay the foundation for exploring what kinds of institutional arrangements lead to the political integration of immigrant interests. While conventional knowledge about the potential influence of the growing immigrant electorate, especially among Latinos, has encouraged state parties and issue-based organizations to target outreach and recruitment among the newly naturalized, these initiatives are episodic with each election cycle rather than sustained attempts at base-building. On the other hand, community organizations, labor unions, and religious institutions — especially urban congregations — have led the way in building a power base among immigrants and across race, class, and ethnicity.[15] The organizing work of these groups goes beyond election season, with a focus on those local and statewide issues in which constituents have a stake. Organizational participation in multi-racial and grassroots activism has impacted local policy outcomes directly affecting immigrant communities. For example, a growing number of local coalitions that link various kinds of organizations around a common policy goal emerged after the passage of the 1996 *Personal Responsibility and Work Opportunities Act* that instituted a Federal five-year bar for recent arrivals.

The grassroots organizing initiatives in the past twenty-five years demonstrate how local political gains are made outside of the electoral arena. The Industrial Areas Foundation (an Alinsky-style federation of community organizations) in Texas and California has had noteworthy political wins through its organizing projects in the Latino communities of Los Angeles and San Antonio (Warren 2001; Shirley 1997; Rogers 1990). Skerry (1993) has describes how these types of mediating institutions enabled and constrained the political integration of

---

[15] For more on the role of religious congregations in organizing, especially through the Industrial Areas Foundation and the Pacific Institute of Community Organizing, see Warren (2001), Wood (2002), Shirley (1997), Pardo (1998), and Rogers (1990).

Mexican Americans, focusing on political regimes that are conducive (or not) to claims-making among minority groups. In that vein, Flores (1997) discusses "cultural citizenship" as a form of engagement among Latino activists whereby excluded groups, regardless of status, aim to reshape society by making demands that are based on issues affecting their daily lives. Similarly, Milkman (2000), Pardo (1998), Shirley (1997), Warren (2001) and Wood (2002) have demonstrated how community-based organizations and networks of groups across race and class have marshaled the political capacity, resources, and power needed for claims-making victories. These forums for political engagement have been training ground for newcomers to acquire skills for civic leadership in their communities. The organizations featured in these studies facilitated connections in the dynamic process of political engagement by mediating group interests with business and government. It is these types of initiatives that have been primary vehicles by which immigrant voices and interests have been brought to bear on current political decision-making processes.

COALITIONS & POLICY CHANGE

As current debates about national immigration reform have grown to a loud crescendo, coalitions of diverse actors have emerged across the country in response to on-going attempts to pass anti-immigrant legislation. In commenting on recent efforts at reform, Tichenor (2002)[16]

---

[16] Tichenor (2002) provides a comprehensive overview of major immigration legislation over six historical periods, examining patterns and variations of policy change and innovation over

concludes that, "not since the early-twentieth century has immigration reform been such a regular focus of conflict and change in American politics" (243). At the heart of this conflict are state and national coalitions attempting to influence legislative outcomes and integrate immigrant interests in policy change.

Attempts at national immigration reform in the last ten years, along with extensive anti-immigrant state laws and local ordinances, have catalyzed a significant grassroots mobilization unseen in this nation.[17] For over a decade, Federal policy initiatives have been aimed at controlling immigration flows into the United States. Border control and restrictions on undocumented immigrants (including increased enforcement) have been the focal point of proposed legislative changes, particularly since the 9/11

---

time (2). This summary is a useful context for the current wave of immigration reform efforts.

[17] A study conducted by Ramakrishnan and Espenshade (2001) found that there is strong link between the presence of anti-immigrant legislation and voting participation among first and second generation immigrants. Their study focused on electoral participation among California's foreign born, naturalized citizens following the 1994 Proposition 187 intended to deny public benefits to undocumented immigrants. They conclude that the presence of anti-immigrant legislation can have profound impact on electoral turnout, and that this finding may indicate a broader lesson about the impact of mobilizing immigrants for electoral participation in the face of anti-immigrant legislation. DeSipio (2002) also found that experiences of discrimination among immigrants are a motivator for civic involvement. Both studies suggest that an anti-immigrant context is a mobilizing factor for political action.

attacks on New York and Washington in 2001. State policy changes have been geared towards limited access to education, health, and social services for local immigrant communities (Singer 2008). Many of these social policy decisions have been left to states since the welfare reforms of 1996.

Most notable among anti-immigrant policy efforts since 2001 was HR 4437, authored by Representative James Sensenbrenner (R-WI). HR 4437 was passed in the House of Representatives in December 2005, targeting undocumented immigrants and those who assist them. The provisions were intended to reduce undocumented immigration, and included new regulations for detention and deportability as well as authorization of state and local police as agents of immigration law (HR 4437; Wang and Winn 2006). Immigrants (both documented and undocumented), service providers, advocates and organizers, and other pro-immigrant allies in Congress and beyond were outraged at this targeted attack. They believed the provisions were harmful to the safety and well-being of *all* immigrants, regardless of legal status. Many activists and advocates attribute the passage of HR 4437 and the growing public awareness of its implications as the catalyst for the marches and rallies that soon followed across the United States (Portes and Rumbaut 2006; Wang and Winn 2006; Viramontes 2008; Ramakrishnan and Bloemraad 2008).

The Spring 2006 immigration marches shocked the nation into a new conversation about the foreign-born in the United States.[18] In their report, "Groundswell meets

---

[18] This report was based on a series of interviews with leaders in the field of immigrant activism. It was intended to capture

Groundwork," Wang and Winn (2006) provide an account of the kinds of organizations involved in this mass mobilization, noting that an organizational infrastructure was already in place to mobilize the millions of people who turned out between March and May 2006. Initiated by a series of informal conversations among pro-immigrant advocates and organizers across the country, these events were, for the most part, peaceful demonstrations with sizable turnouts in Los Angeles, Dallas, New York, and Washington. D.C., where crowd estimates ranged from 100,000 to 500,000 people in each city. The civic message of these events was clear: "*Immigrants are America. Today we march, tomorrow we vote.*"

Wang and Winn suggest that advocates, community groups, local and regional coalitions, and national networks—all of whom have a history and proven track record of working with immigrants— facilitated the groundwork necessary for mass mobilization. The authors posit that it was not indignation at injustice alone that facilitated the mobilization. Rather, the long-standing organizational relationships in immigrant communities and their grassroots' legitimacy coupled with powerful ethnic media outreach made it possible to set in motion a

---

lessons learned from the field, and to make recommendations for funders interested in supporting future grassroots organizing, coalition building, and mobilization. In this regard, the report is pro-immigrant. Counter-point opinions focused primarily on the public issues associated with the protests (legalization, economic impact etc), not the organizational structure and related factors that facilitated the turnout of millions of immigrants.

plan of action within a short time frame (7). They also emphasize that the involvement of additional stakeholders, such as labor unions and religious institutions, especially the Catholic Church, was central to the effectiveness of these mobilizations (8).

Grassroots coalitions have a long tradition of activism for policy change. Countless examples illustrate the benefits and challenges for coalitions of local community groups who advocate a policy agenda rooted in shared commitments to social justice, equity, and fairness (Tarrow 1998). External pressure groups in the policymaking process work to advance their interests by seeking to influence public opinion, agenda setting, and policy decisions (Kingdon 1995). Often motivated by focusing events (Kingdon 1995), grassroots coalitions will engage action strategies that are shaped by their values, interests and policy priorities. The Spring 2006 marches were one such focusing event. Especially in the last twenty years, organizational alliances focused on the rights and interests of immigrants and their families have emerged. These alliances have become a main vehicle through which immigrant political interests are brought into the public arena.

Immigrant coalitions have evolved in formal and informal ways. Service and non-profit organizations have joined forces to address specific public health, social welfare, and education-related issues. Ad hoc groups have built targeted legislative campaigns in response to federal and state health, welfare, and education policy change. State and regional coalitions have formally affiliated to advocate on behalf of smaller ethnic and community-based service organizations. Finally, large networks, predominantly based in Washington D.C. have been established as a legislative presence in national policymaking. These groups and organizations represent the range and diversity of pro-immigrant interests. They employ various strategies for civic engagement including member-based, grassroots organizing, voter education and engagement, and legislative advocacy campaigns around specific issues. Especially at the state level, immigrant coalitions have made gains in influencing policy decisions, and have established themselves as credible and knowledgeable voices on pro-immigrant issues.

Labor unions of predominantly low-wage, foreign-born workers also have become a voice for immigrant interests. Having navigated historic tensions around immigration issues, the Service Employees International Union (SEIU), UNITE HERE, and others have grown their membership base and increased outreach and voter education programs in communities of color. They too have an established presence in Washington D.C. and in many key states, such as California, where immigrant workers comprise the majority of service sector jobs.

Private funders have increasingly promoted collaboration among grantees and supported growth in coalition building for policy change with different kinds of organizational stakeholders. Foundations such as the Four Freedoms Fund, the Knight Foundation and Atlantic Philanthropies have made targeted investments in local immigrant-serving and advocacy organizations.[19] The investments of these foundations coupled with growing efforts at on-the-ground collaboration indicate a

---

[19] See for example a report from The Atlantic Philanthropies, "Why Supporting Advocacy Makes Sense for Foundations," (Deutsch 2008).

movement toward coalition organizing that leverages immigrants' political voice and credibility in ways not yet seen. It is from these initiatives that new knowledge is developing about the organizational mechanisms that facilitate immigrant political incorporation.

COALITION ORGANIZING FOR IMMIGRANT HEALTH CARE

The coalitions that developed around the 2006 marches reveal a political synergy that can exist among immigrant-serving organizations. They demonstrated potential for making political gains when organized around a common concern or shared interested. Individually created for diverse purposes, the organizations involved in the 2006 marches mobilized millions in response to the threat of HR 4437's passage and implementation. On a smaller, yet nonetheless critical scale, these same types of coalitions have been organizing for state policy change. Organizing for health care access has been one social policy issue that cuts across the interests of immigrant rights groups, ethnic organizations, community-based service providers, labor unions, and private foundations.

Access to and affordability of health care is a central public concern for all Americans, not only immigrants and their children. The safety net that once existed to support poor immigrants has been whittled away as more and more states reduce budget allocations for Medicaid, along with funding for local community-based clinics and hospitals that serve this population. With the rising number of uninsured immigrants coupled with growing anti-immigrant hostility, many immigrant-based providers feel they lack the power to make demands and to influence policy decisions that directly affect them, their members, and their communities (Okie 2007; Ku and Papademetriou 2007). As this reality has grown, national organizations like Families USA, SEIU's "Americans for Health Care," and most statewide immigrant advocacy coalitions have organized specifically around this issue. At times, they have allied with health consumer and other grassroots groups in order to leverage political gains, and together have experienced moderate success in protecting the benefits available to immigrants through public programs.

Since the 1996 welfare reform changes, many grassroots networks in states across the country made gains in their fight for immigrant access to public benefits. It is clear that without the active mobilization of these networks and coalitions of community organizations, churches, unions, and service providers, most state-replacement programs would not exist.[20] This example provides the context in which state level coalitions between 2004 and 2007 were investigated. These stories illustrate how coalitions have facilitated the incorporation of immigrant health care interests in the legislative process, and how they have served as one type of contemporary mediating institution.

---

[20] For a case study of Illinois's effort to pass FamilyCare in 2002, see Bouman (2005, 2006). This case explores the successful collaboration between policy advocacy groups and community organizations to win the FamilyCare Campaign, highlighting the necessary role of each organizational type in their policy victory.

CHAPTER THREE

Immigrant Political Power: Claims-making Coalitions and Policy Outcomes

OVERVIEW

Theoretical models about the role of grassroots activism, lobbying, and advocacy coalitions in immigrant political incorporation are not well developed. While individual level analysis has contributed to understanding the pathways of political socialization and civic participation, a less researched area is an examination of organizational factors that impact outcomes. As discussed in Chapter Two, not enough is known about how coalitions of community-based organizations act as intermediary agents of immigrant interests and political power (Ramakrishnan and Bloemraad 2008). How do coalitions negotiate political results on behalf of immigrant interests? In what ways do they facilitate direct participation and grassroots leadership? What types of organizational arrangements facilitate successful policy outcomes? These questions were central to the investigation of coalition activity in Massachusetts and California between 2004 and 2007, and under-gird the theory that developed out of the findings (Eisenhardt and Graebner 2007).

This inquiry began with the proposition that immigrant political incorporation is contingent on the ability of immigrants 1) to build political capacity through organizations and 2) to act effectively on behalf of their interests by exercising public influence through demand making. The preliminary hypothesis was that these two factors — political capacity and public influence — would impact the coalitions' ability to win their policy demands. As an exploratory investigation designed to build a theoretical framework (Eisenhardt and Graebner 2007), this formulation evolved over the course of the research project (Ragin 1994). Through the case analysis, one model for understanding successful incorporation of immigrant interests in policy change was found to depend on 1) inter-organizational partnerships in the coalition building process, 2) intra-organizational development (or the internal capacity building of skills, resources, and constituencies) and 3) influence within the public and legislative context. Table 2 presents the three central constructs and the analytic questions posed in the study to develop the theoretical framework.

Together, this theoretical framework points to a set of conditions under which coalitions in the policymaking process can increase capacity and grassroots power, as well as influence policy change. Certainly, context shapes whether or not coalitions can acquire and mobilize the capacity to accomplish their goals: both organizational and environmental factors give rise to the relationships and power necessary for success. The framework that results from this study explains one approach to understanding how coalitions are an inter-organizational mechanism for mediating the political interests of immigrants within the

TABLE 2: Theoretical Framework
Coalition organizing to influence state health policy affecting immigrants and their children

Theoretical Constructs	Analytic Questions
Political Capacity	In what ways do coalition building and internal organizational development increase the political capacity of organizations to take public action?
1. Inter-organizational development	How do inter-organizational relationships facilitate or inhibit effective coalition building?
2. Intra-organizational development	How does coalition building facilitate or inhibit intra-organizational development among coalition partner organizations?
Public Influence	In what ways do community-based coalitions wield influence through public action?
3. Claims-making	Are policy goals achieved? How does the coalition participate in the legislative process?
Political Incorporation of Immigrant Interests	To what extent do coalitions successfully bring immigrant interests to the policymaking environment?

policy arena. Central to this theoretical model are the interactions between coalition formation, grassroots campaigns for policy change, and the outcomes of such processes within in a policymaking context.

INTER-ORGANIZATIONAL DEVELOPMENT: COALITION BUILDING

Claims-making coalitions are purposive, voluntary, inter-organizational partnerships (Oliver 1990) that rely on the resources, ideology, and power of its members to accomplish goals (Mizrahi and Rosenthal 2001; Roberts-DeGennaro and Mizrahi 2005; Levi and Murphy 2006). Roberts-DeGennaro and Mizrahi (2005) describe such coalitions as a tool for social change in the following way:

> Coalition building is a strategy for social action that can bring together diverse organizations to advocate for reform in the structural arrangements for delivering and accessing health care, education, social welfare, and other human services. In addition, coalitions can influence political, social, and economic forces that affect the development of policies and services. In advocating for social change, coalitions orchestrate a diverse range of tactics and techniques from consensus to conflict (305).

Levi and Murphy (2006) differentiate between those coalitions that are formed for a specific "event" (such as a protest) and those that are "enduring," with more formal structures, a long-term purpose, established principles, and pooled resources (655). Mizrahi and Rosenthal (2001) further distinguish between inter-organizational partnerships for collaborative service delivery and those intended to achieve shared claims-making goals.[21] Claims-making coalitions (also known as advocacy coalitions) are a widely used strategy of inter-organizational alliances that intend to make demands on an external political entity. Likewise, alliances that form without a political action agenda per se,[22] may at some point make use of claims-making coalitions as a strategy for social change. In both instances, they are a vehicle by which grassroots and advocacy partners join forces around common interests, combine resources, and organize for specific policy changes that meet shared goals (Mizrahi and Rosenthal 2001; Hojnacki 1998; Mondros and Wilson 1994; McAdam, McCarthy, and Zald 1996).

Coalition initiatives for claims-making purposes are shaped by the local public policy context. Forging alliances among non-profit and grassroots organizations is a widespread practice in local and metropolitan areas. Within a common context (i.e. scale of population, scope of issues), organizations are able to leverage broader support

---

[21] While both types of coalitions contain common factors that influence effectiveness and outcomes, those with an expressed goal of demand making is the focus of this study. See Zakocs and Edwards (2006) for review of literature on coalition building factors and indicators of effectiveness in community coalitions for health promotion and delivery.

[22] For example, Waddock and Post (1995) argue that "catalytic alliances" are inter-organizational networks in which organizations share overlapping interests, unite around a core vision, and combine resources for the purpose of mobilizing public action on a social problem (959). The authors cite the Partnership for a Drug-Free America and Hands Across America as examples of such alliances.

for community initiatives. Attempts to organize statewide advocacy coalitions add to the complexity of inter-organizational partnerships intended to make claims on government. Geography, diversity of population, variation in socio-political, economic and cultural concerns, and the scope of work (breadth and depth) each present challenges that impact the nature and effectiveness of organizing at this level (Reynolds 2004; Roberts-DeGennaro and Mizrahi 2005). As Fred Rose (2004) argues, "coalitions are not just political instruments, but also complex social relationships that emerge from historic events based on the predispositions, understandings, values and commitments of participants" (11).

Partnering organizations navigate these complex relationships in order to build effective inter-organizational alliances. They have to agree to a common agenda, goals, strategy, and tactics that meet their diverse, and at times, competing interests (Rose 2004). Agreements of this nature are a primary challenge for large-scale policy coalitions. They can require extensive negotiation and collaboration that will undoubtedly push the boundaries of trust and cooperation. Coalition organizing can also be an opportunity to transcend each organization's individual interests to a mutually agreed upon agenda and strategy for action (Reynolds 2004; Roberts-DeGennaro and Mizrahi 2005).[23]

---

[23] Reynolds (2004) examines various labor-community coalitions and summarizes three central challenges to coalition building: breadth, depth, and agenda. These conclusions are well matched to the challenges identified in the coalitions in Massachusetts and California.

Inter-organizational alliances form for a variety of reasons. Oliver (1990) suggests that six general "contingencies" can explain what causes organizations to form relationships: necessity (of voluntary or mandated agreement), asymmetry (of control and resources), reciprocity (in pursuing common or mutually beneficial goals), efficiency (of output and resource maximization), stability and predictability (in the operating environment), and legitimacy (to increase external reputation and image). While one contingency can be sufficient for establishing a relationship, many organizational partnerships are based on multiple contingencies (246). When this broad framework ·is applied to social change coalitions, the contingencies help explain how and why organizational alliances form initially, how they grow and behave over time, and the extent to which they can achieve their intended goals (Oliver 1990). For example in Levi and Murphy's (2006) examination of event coalitions, specific factors were found to "make or break" an alliance (652). According to the authors, shared framing and resources are necessary but not sufficient conditions for coalition formation and sustainability. They conclude that elements such as pre-existing trust relationships and formalized institutional arrangements (i.e. coalition rules) also will impact cooperation, commitment, and members' ability to manage inter-organizational tension (658).

Subject to relational dynamics among partners as well as external forces in the operating environment, inter-organizational alliances will evolve and change over time (Sharfman, Gray, and Yan 1991; Mizrahi and Rosenthal 2001). A coalition balances a host of internal and external forces that have the potential to hamper its goals and strategies for action (Roberts-DeGennaro and Mizrahi

2005). Once established, coalition strength and effectiveness depend upon core elements within the coalition itself such as a common public concern, shared organizational commitment, the structure of relationships, and the scope and scale of coalition activity (Tattersall and Reynolds 2007). In their review of the literature on public health coalitions, Zakocs and Edwards (2006) identified other factors that are positively associated with coalition effectiveness including: formalized rules, leadership style, active member participation, member diversity, collaboration, and group cohesion (356-7).[24] These elements will either contribute to or impede a coalition's sustainability, which will ultimately impact its ability to achieve its intended goals (Tattersall and Reynolds 2007). Therefore, success in coalition organizing will be a function of both internal factors and the circumstances outside of the coalition itself (such as political opposition or abrupt changes in legislative activity).

Successful inter-organizational coalitions unite around a shared vision and a common agreement of goals, priorities, and action strategies (Tattersall and Reynolds 2007; Roberts-DeGennaro and Mizrahi 2005). With a heterogeneous group of organizational partners that represent a diverse constituency, the coalition has access to a range of skills and resources needed for effective

---

[24] Zakocs and Edwards' (2006) review of the literature on collaborative coalitions highlights that there is significant variation in measurement of coalition building factors and indicators of effectiveness. Though the focus of their review was not on research of claims-making coalitions, the findings on the internal workings of coalitions are applicable and relevant to the framework explored here.

collaborative work to make claims in the public arena (Foster-Fishman et al. 2001, 250). High levels of competency among core leadership enable tensions to be managed. For example, effective coalition leaders are able to balance unity with diversity, promote accountability, and motivate commitment to the coalition while facilitating member autonomy and loyalty to their own organizational purposes (Roberts-DeGennaro and Mizrahi 2005, 309). The interdependent nature of a coalition can lead to greater political power and influence for change by coalescing its internal, collaborative capacity for action (Foster-Fishman et al. 2001; Hojnacki 1998; Ganz 2008). Collective work through coalitions can increase the resource capacity of each member organization: new organizational structures may emerge; organizers and staff acquire new skills; new leadership and members are recruited to the organization. Together, this intra-organizational development strengthens individual organizations, which will subsequently strengthen the overall coalition.

INTRA-ORGANIZATIONAL DEVELOPMENT

As members in a coalition, it is possible for organizations to develop new internal capacities that would not necessarily result from activities within its own boundaries. Invariably, participation in a coalition impacts individual organizations (Roberts-DeGennaro and Mizrahi 2005). In the same way that Oliver's (1990) framework of contingencies guides an analysis of why coalitions form, it also helps to identify the extent to which these partnerships impact participating members. Whether they are formally or informally established, inter-organizational relationships are not "cost-free" for members (Oliver 1990).

Coalition members make choices about the potential advantages and disadvantages to the organization when committing to joint goals rather than focusing solely on one's own internal goals and priorities. Even if there is significant efficiency and effectiveness at the coalition level, there also may be considerable depletion of resources among individual units (Roberts-DeGennaro and Mizrahi 2005).

On the other hand, coalition-level effectiveness may lead to enhanced intra-organizational development. An organization's member base or staff may be engaged in carrying out its mission and programs in new ways; organizing skills may be newly developed or honed; and new relationships may evolve and be mobilized in ways that advance individual goals and priorities along with the shared goals of the coalition.[25] These outcomes may depend on several conditions including: the extent to which campaign goals, strategies, and actions are aligned with organizational priorities; how well coordinated and useful the campaign's actions are to the organizations; and whether or not staff and leaders are able to facilitate feedback loops of learning and evaluation about the organization's work within the coalition.[26]

Alliances are interactive by their nature. As a result, individual organizations may rearticulate goals and strategic priorities; they may develop new internal skills as they work in new contexts; they may access new resources that not only enhance the agenda and actions of the alliance, but also strengthen their internal functioning;

[25] See Peterson (2004) for more on the related concepts of "deep organizing," membership involvement, and commitment.

[26] For more on coalition effectiveness, see Stone (1989, 210-212).

they may develop new methods for managing day-to-day operations and tapping into the skills and resources of their own organizational stakeholders. Expanding an organization's scope of work beyond its defined boundaries can, in turn, lead to organizational change. In some cases, the additional commitment of participation in an alliance may exhaust organizational resources (Roberts-DeGennaro and Mizrahi 2005). For others, it may be an opportunity to strengthen and enhance the internal capacity of that organization. These dimensions of change are all indicators of intra-organizational development that can occur through coalition participation.

Coalitions can be a constructive organizational form for linking local resources to larger campaigns that address public issues of concern. When a community-based organization is directly connected to the issue at hand, it is likely to initiate involvement or be called upon to join a cause. The investment an organization makes will reflect this motivation and its level of commitment. For example, an organization that is deeply connected to the mission and everyday work of the coalition may devote extensive resources, staff time, and people power to a policy campaign, whereas one that signs-on as an endorser may not be as motivated to make the same level of commitment (Hojnacki 1998). Along with its motivation and self-interest, an organization's involvement may be limited by the availability of resources or the relationships it does and does not have with potential partner groups in the alliance. Even among small organizations, when an organization commits staff, money, and time, it indicates a degree of ownership in the coalition and a desire to achieve multiple goals. (Hojnacki 1998; Tattersall and Reynolds 2007; Clawson 2003). This is yet another way to measure how a coalition impacts individual organizations: the benefits of participation are likely to go beyond potential policy change, especially for those organizations without much political clout that are able to connect with more powerful organizations.

CLAIMS-MAKING SUCCESS

A key dimension of identifying how inter-organizational alliances have public influence is to examine their success. Coalition success can include a range of outcomes, including achieving policy objectives, establishing long-term relationships with allies, and increasing decision makers' awareness of and responsiveness to the implications of an issue (Hojnacki 1998, 441). For coalitions of community-based organizations—including those with the expressed purpose of demand making—internal achievements and failures hold significance (Mizrahi and Rosenthal 2001). The dynamics within an alliance as well as those external to the coalition can affect claims-making success.[27]   Mizrahi and Rosenthal (2001) found that even though external factors played a critical role in coalition success, organizers and coalition leaders perceived that internal factors were just as significant in the success or failure of a coalition.

That said, to make substantial public policy gains, a coalition needs to influence those with the power to decide *and* win on the issues. Effectiveness and viability hinge upon the coalition's ability to establish a reputation for being a credible source on matters affecting their

---

[27] See also Crowley et. al, (2007) for discussion of what constitutes success in "organizations of the poor." The authors draw useful parallels to the measures of success discussed here.

constituencies. Coalition leaders with an ongoing voice in the policymaking process are able to expand their participation from occasional contributions to the policy debate to more regular involvement and interaction with policymakers. Where achieving one's policy goals is a primary indicator of success, active participation in agenda setting and perceived credibility among legislators are also important measures of a group's ability to have influence in the public arena (Sabatier 2007; Sabatier and Jenkins-Smith 1993; Kingdom 1995). Even when there is defeat, having new allies in the legislature, developing an organized public presence at hearings, demonstrating knowledge and resources available to legislative staff, and mobilizing voters are dimensions of successfully influencing demands.

POLITICAL CAPACITY & INFLUENCE IN THE PUBLIC ARENA

Non-profit and community-based organizations that work with immigrants confront a host of social, economic, and cultural concerns that are inherently political. Whether they intend to or not, these organizations often find themselves in political roles. Even the smallest of organizations will, at certain times, span the boundary between maintaining day-to-day operations and the need to take on more public, and subsequently more political, roles in the communities in which they operate (De Graauw 2008; Schmid-Thomas 1993). Because they tend to be deeply embedded within these communities, direct, hands-on experiences inform their actions in the public arena. One critical element of their success when attempting to influence change is the inter- and intra-organizational development of a coalition and its members.   The examples explored in Chapter Five highlight factors that explain how coalitions achieve success in this regard.

Bolman and Deal's (1997, 2008) "political frame" provides one avenue for understanding the position of immigrant-serving organizations within a public policy context. They argue that organizations are political units, and contain a complex web of individual and group interests that are negotiated through an intentional process of bargaining, conflict, and power. They further suggest that organizations are "both arenas for internal politics and political agents with their own agendas, resources and strategies," operating within complicated ecosystems where competition, collaboration, and interdependence are all factors that influence action (Bolman and Deal 1997, 210-211).[28]   As a result, organizations need capacity not only to confront internal negotiations of power and resources, but also to participate as political actors beyond organizational boundaries, negotiating conflict and having influence on the concerns that directly matter to them.

One central assumption of social network theory is the notion that relationships shape organizational behavior (Nohria   and   Eccles   1992;   Granovetter   1973).

---

[28]While Bolman and Deal's theoretical framework has broad applicability to organizations across sectors, the political frame has particularly relevance here to the structures and dynamics within organizational networks created for political power. In their 4th edition of *Reframing Organizations: Artistry, Choice and Leadership* (2008), Bolman and Deal develop this idea further and emphasize organizations as coalitions of individuals and groups who negotiate power and conflict, compete for scarce resources, and bargain for power and authority.

Organizational interactions influence internal goals and priorities, strategies, and decision-making. Information, knowledge, and control flow between interactions, often through interdependent exchange (Powell 1990). The relative strength or weakness of these connections makes it possible for an organization to carry out its mission, to conduct its routine operations, and to respond to pressures for action (Weick 1976; Granovetter 1973). Trust, commitment, and reputation will affect the nature of relationships in and between organizations, and tend to influence whether or not those relationships will last over time (Powell 1990). When mere interactions become relationships rooted in shared purposes, they can expand knowledge and information, enhance day-to-day operations, and inform organizational goals, priorities, and strategies.

This orientation to organizational behavior sheds light on the dynamics of political capacity in coalitions. It is the exchanges within relational networks—both formal and informal—that can become a source of inter-organizational capacity for public action and power. Consequently, exchanges within relational networks can yield increased capacity of individual organizational actors. Alliances among non-profit and community organizations can build the overall capacity of the group so that it has the power to accomplish shared goals otherwise not achievable alone. When inter-organizational partnerships emerge in response to political opportunities and threats, the combined organizational capacity that results from relational networks becomes a critical ingredient for successful outcomes.

Whether organizing for collaborative purposes (as in coalitions for service delivery) or for demand making (as in social change coalitions), organizations identify, gather, and mobilize the resources necessary for action, especially through relationship building. Political capacity grows as organizations work together over time, develop trust and cooperation, respond to shared goals with strategic purpose, and challenge situations of dependency and domination (Roberts-DeGennaro and Mizrahi 2005; Ganz 2000). With this kind of growth, the organizations themselves are better equipped to take public action. In rapidly changing political environments, individual organizations depend on, but often lack, the structures and internal processes that allow for adaptability, while maintaining adherence to their core mission, values, and responsibilities. Adaptability to complex and fluid environments is contingent on those organizational structures that facilitate or constrain an organization's ability to develop and mobilize power for action through relationships (Mondros and Wilson 1994). In coalitions, this adaptability coupled with adherence to shared mission, is critical to achieving intended outcomes.

Therefore, political capacity in organizations is integral to successful political outcomes.[29] Some organizations — precisely because of their organizational design, mission, and goals — take on the role of political actor in the public arena. They fit naturally into this arena and have an explicit infrastructure for responding to political events.

---

[29] Many definitions of "political" can be drawn from across the disciplines. To simplify, my assumption here is that "political" is used to capture the interactive process of influence, power, decision-making, and control between government and external organizations as well as among and within organizations themselves.

Others function almost exclusively outside of this realm, such as the many small-size mutual aid associations that serve the direct needs of immigrants and their families (De Graauw 2008; Applied Research Center 2002). However, those organizations outside any formal political environment may, at times, be forced to respond to unexpected opportunities or targeted threats that affect their mission and goals, interests, and activities (Craig, Taylor, and Parkes 2004; Rakich and Feit 2001; Jackson-Elmoore 2005). Focusing events as defined by Kingdon (1995) propel organizations from their usual routines into a broader public role (Tarrow 1998). Regardless of the source, needed institutional responses to focusing events often catapult organizations into arenas of political action and controversy.

It is more likely today that well-resourced lobbyists, sophisticated interest groups, and highly organized constituencies access public officials, contribute to policy agenda setting, build public pressure for change, and participate in implementation strategies. Yet, citizen participation can make a difference in public policymaking (Sirianni 2009; De Souza Briggs 2008; Taylor 2003). Skocpol (1999) comments that social movement leaders have been "vital agents of democratic revitalization" (467), but that the landscape of civic engagement has changed dramatically. This has been especially true because of what Skocpol (1999) argues is the "advocacy explosion," the transformation of associational life in the United States from membership-based to advocacy-oriented institutions. As argued in the previous chapter, community-based organizations, civic and ethnic associations, and grassroots advocacy groups have direct experiences in communities that typically are not involved in public decision making.[30] Because of this, these organizations can be agents of group interests that might otherwise remain outside the boundaries of public decision-making and government. For communities without considerable representation or voice, claims-making coalitions can be a critical entrée into democratic life and a source of power building. The examples found in Chapter Five explore how a contemporary form of coalition organizing has advanced the political interests of one such group.

---

[30] Some scholarship of the last fifteen years has examined how communities of color access the policymaking process, though this research is limited and lends itself to further case study investigation (McClain 1993).

CHAPTER FOUR

Research Design for Theory and Practice

OVERVIEW

This project used case study methods to investigate a current policy event and the related organizational processes of coalitions attempting to influence that policy. Its central research question was: *How do statewide coalitions facilitate the incorporation of immigrant interests in state health policy change?* The main purpose of the research was to develop a theoretical framework that explains what role intermediary groups — in this instance, coalitions — play in immigrant political incorporation. Using exploratory case methods, the research objectives were two-fold: 1) to improve the tools scholars use to analyze organizational processes that explain the incorporation of immigrant interests in policy change; and 2) to illuminate best practices for practitioners engaged in this work (Eisenhardt and Graebner 2007).

Multiple sources of data were used to construct individual case narratives that explain how and why coalitions in each state facilitated the incorporation of immigrant health interests (among other policy goals) into state health policy changes made between 2004 and 2007. The research examined the organizational processes of the coalitions, the nature of the public actions taken, and the outcomes of such activities. This method also allowed for an analysis of how and why certain external factors, or the contextual variables, may have impacted organizational process and outcomes.

An initial case study was conducted in Massachusetts immediately following the passage of statewide health reform. With the addition of the California case, a cross-case analysis was conducted of how statewide coalitions were built, how they organized themselves for political action, and how they made demands for health policy change that specifically affected immigrants and their families. The purpose of this analysis was 1) to determine what organizational factors contribute to coalition success, and 2) to develop a theoretical model for understanding such processes. The findings presented in this book explain how the inter-organizational base of power built by coalition partners was an effective mechanism for demand making even though there were different kinds of policy success. As with other case studies, the set of findings from Massachusetts and California are particular to the examples investigated, and its strength is found in its applicability to new ideas that can lead to future empirical work (George and Bennett 2005; Ragin 1994; Eisenhardt and Graebner 2007; Reinharz 1992).

BACKGROUND

I initially set out to study how grassroots organizations engage immigrant communities in political action. Informed by my observations as a practitioner in this setting, I pursued scholarly research on the role of organizations in immigrant political participation, and found that only a handful of researchers had examined immigrant political involvement through the lens of organizational impact on policy change. I then began to investigate current examples of organizations engaging in policy change work that would be suitable cases for the inquiry (Reinharz 1992). In particular, I wanted to locate examples that would provide data from which I could build a theoretical model for future empirical work (Ragin 1994; Eisenhardt 1989). I narrowed the focus to state-level cases where coalitions of community organizations have attempted to change social policies that affect immigrants. I formulated research questions out of this background investigation, and determined that the most effective methodological approach for developing an applicable theory would be an analysis of state-level examples.

One difference between case study research and other forms of scientific inquiry is its direct application for practitioners. Case studies can appeal to wider audiences who will make use of findings in their every day practice (Eisenhardt and Graebner 2007; Yin 2003). Beyond strong adherence to the techniques central to case study methods, Yin (2003) notes that exemplary case studies present evidence of a revelatory phenomenon, are of interest in the general public, or investigate issues of central importance to theory, policy, and/or practice. These dimensions of case methods remained central to the research objectives.

RATIONALE

As the interdisciplinary study of immigrant political incorporation grows, case study investigations have been found to be a valuable tool for advancing theoretical understandings (Ramakrishnan and Bloemraad 2008; Però and Solomos 2010). Case study research is an effective methodology for examining current phenomena and building theory about such events out of a structured, focused analysis (George and Bennett 2005; Yin 2003). With this method, the researcher can conduct an in-depth analysis of historically significant events by evaluating the dynamic interactions among individuals, groups, institutions, and systems (George and Bennett 2005; Ragin 1994; Yin 2003). Theory can be developed in case studies when ideas about a particular phenomenon are connected to the facts of a case with rich empirical evidence from several data sources (Eisenhardt and Graebner 2007; Ragin 1994). Theoretical conclusions are drawn then from the inferences made about the relationships between the main analytic factors and the outcomes observed in a given case (Eisenhardt and Graebner 2007; Ragin 1994; Yin 2003).

Case study methods are most appropriate for research that investigates "how and why" questions (Yin 2003). George and Bennett (2005) argue that, "case study researchers are more interested in finding the conditions under which specified outcomes occur, and the mechanisms through which they occur, rather than uncovering the frequency with which those conditions and their outcomes arise" (31). This analytic focus is coupled with methods that allow for more in-depth examination of how context contributes to factors influencing the outcomes of a given case. George and Bennett (2005) also claim that case study research is a valuable strategy for examining policy-relevant problems and that, with this method, the researcher can accommodate complex relationships. Though this may produce narrower generalizations about a given phenomenon, it allows the researcher to consider possible contingencies that lead to outcomes, to account for those contexts in which a given case occurs, and to illuminate theory that is germane to practice (George and Bennett 2005; Ragin 1994).

Finally, case study research has been used widely to develop theory (Eisenhardt and Graebner 2007; George and Bennett 2005). All case studies, including exploratory ones, should be rooted in a theoretical framework that guides the research design, the development of new ideas and analytic frames, and the investigation of relevant evidence to support those ideas (Ragin 1994; Yin 2003). Yin (2003) describes theoretical propositions as a "blueprint" for case studies. These propositions are developed at the outset of a research project. They serve as the theoretical foundation from which data is collected and analyzed, and from which constructs are reevaluated based on findings. Case study design also allows for flexibility and revisions as the research process unfolds. It may be that a first case in a multiple case study reveals new information or inadequacies in the initial design that can be adjusted for in subsequent cases (Yin 2003). Without shifting the research objective, the researcher can and should modify the design to more closely align the investigation with its intended goals (Yin 2003, 55). Especially for research questions where there is no existing theory or where the theory that does exist is insufficient, the strong emphasis on carefully articulated and intentionally analyzed theoretical propositions makes case methods a useful tool for developing new ways of understanding complex social and political phenomena.

METHODS
This project was guided by the proposition that immigrant political incorporation is contingent on the ability of newcomers to build political capacity through

organizations and to act on behalf of their interests by exercising public influence through demand-making. This central assumption framed the case study methods employed in the investigation of factors present in the organizational processes of coalition building as well as the external context of that process.

Unit of Analysis & Case Selection
Given the scope of the research inquiry and the primary case focus on activity in two states, data collection was concentrated at the level of organizations, with coalitions of organizations as the central unit of analysis. A sub-unit of analysis was the individual member organizations that worked with an immigrant constituency. Yin (2003) recommends that in defining the unit of analysis, a specific time boundary for the case must also be determined. This boundary framed the context in which cases were selected and data was collected and analyzed. The analysis accounts for those conditions prior to and following data collection, but maintains as its focus the processes and outcomes of the time period studied.

The coalitions in each state were selected because of their known and active participation in organizing around health policy issues. The goal of selection was to locate examples that would provide rich data and that could yield the strongest possible analytic inferences about the propositions guiding the research inquiry (George and Bennett 2005). This process began with a focus on those states where current access to health benefits for immigrants was in question. A scan of state legislative history following welfare reform provided a preliminary list of states to target for participation (Fremstad and Cox 2004). Because systematic information about organizing efforts proved difficult to find, national immigrant organizations were consulted for guidance. It was essential to identify crucial cases that could illustrate a range of factors explaining the outcomes for investigation (George and Bennett 2005; Ragin 1994; Siggelkow 2007).

Case selection was guided by four criteria. Keeping state-level, health policy change constant across examples, organizations and coalitions that had or were in the midst of organizing a statewide campaign for health policy change affecting immigrants were identified. Second, cases with similarities in the operating environment were identified. These characteristics included a common overarching policy arena and a mix of organizational types involved in the coalition (i.e. policy, advocacy, and grassroots organizing partner groups). Variations in the operating environment were inevitable (George and Bennett 2005). For this study, variation was expected in the state's geographic scope and population demographics, the nature of the state's political institutions, and the history of organizational relationships. Though quite different in this regard, coalitions in Massachusetts and California were also at the forefront of active mobilization for state health policy change. This made them ideal for investigation (Siggelkow 2007).

A third criteria involved organizational structure and processes that would provide points of variation. These included coalition leadership structure, funding sources, internal decision-making structures, relationship to a national or statewide organization, and types of organizing strategies for political action. The final criteria was whether or not several groups of main actors would be available to provide rich detail about the coalitions, organizational members, and the campaign through in-depth interviews.

Selection bias is a considerable and realistic concern when using case study research. To account for potential bias in this study, I sought cases that would be, first and foremost, crucial cases to guide the development of theory. Another advantage of the case study method is the opportunity to investigate those cases where there is variation in both the outcomes and the factors influencing that outcome. Though I was not testing hypotheses, I accounted for this potential threat to validity in the case selection process. I identified examples where the organizational processes were similar enough so as to minimize variation across the cases and increase the explanatory power of the analysis.

Data Collection
Two phases of data collection were conducted in each state, beginning with Massachusetts in March 2006, and adding California in July 2006. Phase One focused on gathering background information about the context of the organizing effort. It included an examination of relevant public policies related to immigrant health care and of the policy and organizational contexts in which the campaigns took place. Preliminary analysis of this data focused on identifying environmental conditions that shaped the external circumstances under which organizations formed coalitions and took public action. This analysis contextualized the investigation of how and why the coalitions attempted to advocate for changes in state health policies for immigrants and their children, and guided the protocol for interviews conducted in Phase Two of the data collection. This protocol was based on an initial set of

organizational factors identified as possible explanations for successful organizing, coalition building, and demand making.

Using in-depth, semi-structured interviews with key informants, Phase Two of data collection examined how and why organizations were involved in their respective organizing campaigns. The main focus of this phase was to explain the organizational processes that led groups to organize in coalitions around health care policy, and the dynamics that unfolded through the phases of public action. Interviews were targeted to the leaderships of member organizations and coalitions, especially those with ties to immigrants. Some front-line staff members directly involved in organizing were also interviewed. Key informant interviews initially expanded the respondent pool using snowball methods, asking respondents to name additional knowledgeable individuals. Interviews with first and second-generation immigrants were limited to organizers or staff of immigrant service or advocacy groups that were main actors in the coalitions.[31] Interviews covered the following areas:

1. Why organizational partners organized around the health policy issue and why they joined the coalition;
2. What happened during the campaign and what were the key strategic/decision-making events;

---

[31] Due to limitations of time and access, I was unable to employ a parallel system with policymakers in the State legislature and executive branches. Conducting an in-depth examination of the perceptions of state policy-makers using the theoretical model developed could expand the research findings.

3. How they coordinated coalition activity and constituent mobilization;
4. Whether or not the organizing campaign led to its intended claims-making outcomes; and
5. Informants' assessment of impact internally (to the organization and its main constituency) and externally (among partner organizations and in State legislature).

During this phase of data collection, I attended and observed public meetings to which respondents invited me. I wrote field notes following each interview or site visit, compiling periodic analytic memos to capture findings as they emerge. I gathered additional secondary documents obtained through public use on the Internet and those given to me by respondents. These secondary documents were collected systematically (ordered by site, coalition, and organization), and this material informed the coalition descriptions used during the analysis phase (Huberman and Miles 1994). In-person interviews were recorded digitally upon permission from the respondent and then transcribed for analysis. Phone interviews were not recorded digitally, but type-written notes were taken. Respondents were assured of their anonymity, and confidentiality was guaranteed prior to conducting the interviews and observing coalition meetings. As a result, no direct quotations have been reported.

Using the analytic categories described in Table 3, transcripts, field-notes, analytic memos, and secondary documents were examined for common themes, experiences, and insights regarding the main study questions (Lofland and Lofland 1995; Maxwell 2005, Eisenhardt 1989). In addition, supplementary questions that emerged in the course of the study were explored in greater depth during later stages of the investigation. This iterative process proved to be particularly useful as data collection in Massachusetts was finalized, and the inquiry in California began (Eisenhardt 1989; Eisenhardt and Graebner 2007). Upon completion of data collection in California, I returned to the Massachusetts case and pursued points of similarity and difference in the examples.[32]

The analytic categories described in Table 3 framed the interview coding. Once interviews were conducted and coded, the initial categories were reordered and integrated, refining the analytic categories throughout the analysis process. This method allowed for the addition, removal, and grouping of categories as data was gathered. Field and analytic memos were critical in guiding this process of coding and re-categorization as needed. Regular discussions about the data with colleagues also informed the final set of categories used for the analysis.

Interview Protocol
Semi-structured interview protocols were used in each state. Question probes were reserved and asked only if spontaneous responses failed to address key analytical points (Lofland and Lofland 1995). With this approach, informants were asked general questions pertaining to the analytic categories described in Table 3. They were encouraged to provide all information that they believe relevant to the issue. Each interview also contained a number of potential follow-up or probe questions. If the

---

[32] In preparing this text for publication, I returned to key informants between 2009 and 2010 to update the final sections of each narrative.

spontaneous responses did not answer the probe question, more detailed questions were then asked. This approach was intended to maximize the practical knowledge of respondents and assure that all explanatory categories were touched upon. Sample interview protocols are included in Appendix 1.

Using this approach, a systematic feedback loop existed through which new categories of questions were added as respondents introduced previously unconsidered explanations. In both field and analytic memos, I noted information spontaneously provided versus information that was obtained via probes and pre-determined analytic categories. This helped to distinguish between academic explanatory categories and those that were used operationally by the practitioners interviewed. This method resulted in the development of new analytic categories that were then incorporated into the investigation and analysis. Having both, and being able to compare them, has allowed the findings to have wider application in the practitioner community and is reflected in the recommendations developed in the concluding chapter.

Analysis

One advantage of using case study methods is that it affords the researcher systematic procedures needed for in-depth analysis of a given phenomenon, and provides mechanisms by which she can account for the complexity of context and multiple explanations of outcomes (George and Bennett 2005). According to Yin (2003) one goal of a study with more than one case is "to build a general explanation that fits each of the individual cases, even though the cases will vary in their details" (121). Case analysis is strengthened—even in exploratory studies—when initial propositions are reevaluated based on evidence from the cases (Eisenhardt and Graebner 2007; Yin 2003). The cross-case analysis in this project is the result of a series of iterations in which the facts of each case were analyzed and compared with the initial propositions. These theoretical ideas were then revised, and, in comparing coalition activity in each state, revised again (Yin 2003). This systematic map was the foundation for the analysis found in Chapter Six.

The findings are based on an analysis of both process and outcomes: the organizational processes of the coalitions were analyzed first and the outcomes of those processes in each example were then evaluated. To begin, I developed the narratives of coalition activity in each state (found in Chapter Five). The narratives focus specifically on the dimensions of coalition organizing and public policy change related to immigrant health coverage. They were constructed using information from both phases of data collection, along with available newspaper accounts of public events (though these proved to be limited). A timeline and organizational map for each case also guided the development of the narratives. These analytic tools were compiled using the multiple data sources described above.

The process analysis of each case involved three stages. First, interview transcripts were coded using the analytic categories and subcategories described in Table 3. Field notes, analytic memos, and secondary documents were reviewed for additional data that either supported or refuted the evidence found in each analytic category. During this review, additional memos were written based on preliminary findings for each state. The focus of this process analysis was the dynamics between coalition partners (inter-organizational development), and within individual member organizations (intra-organizational development). Organizational processes were examined in this way to better fit the study's main questions about understanding a process of change. Particular attention was paid to how those conditions internal to the member organizations interacted with the operating environment, both in the coalitions as well as within the policy arena (Lawrence and Lorsch 1967).

Similarly, an analysis of outcomes was conducted and was intended to articulate indicators of successful coalition organizing and demand making. As described in Chapter Three, the literature on community organizing stresses that the political activities of grassroots advocacy and organizing groups can yield success in a variety of ways: it is not defined solely by the claims-making outcomes of a given campaign. Other forms of success may also include developing new grassroots leadership, creating more durable organizational structures for long-term sustainability, building stronger partnerships with other organizations or government agencies, and establishing collaborative power within the coalition that did not exist prior to a campaign. Even if the intended claims-making goals are not met, these factors can contribute to future action. Based on this premise, an initial set of "success indicators" were included in the coding structure and embedded as subcategories within the analytic format. In this regard, there was overlap between the process and outcomes analysis.

The cross-case analysis was conducted once the analysis of coalitions in each state was completed. The analytic format found in Table 3 again provided the foundation from which cases were evaluated for similarities and differences. Background research completed during Phase One provided a context for the comparative analysis. This enabled the findings to be situated within a broader conversation about immigrant coalition building and grassroots mobilization for public policy change. The first analysis of the Massachusetts case completed in December 2006 was the basis for the larger theory-building analysis. The categories were refined as a result of the findings from Massachusetts as well as the analytic memos written during data collection in California. This revision of the analytic format increased the explanatory power of the findings in the comparison. Categories were formulated inductively to reflect the integration of predetermined factors with factors that were identified by respondents as significant in the coalition process and campaign outcomes.

Reliability & Validity

High levels of concept validity are possible with case studies (George and Bennett 2005). With them, the researcher can determine valid and reliable indicators "that best represent the theoretical concepts the research intends to measure" (George and Bennett 2005, 19). For each example in this study, multiple forms of evidence from different data sources reinforced connections between the theoretical framework and the analysis of the findings (Eisenhardt and Graebner 2007). Reliability was drawn from interviews with a variety of actors involved in each organizing campaign, and feedback loops were used with participants and organizations to verify the data collected. The iterative process of determining analytic categories and analyzing evidence also ensured validity of the findings (Eisenhardt and Graebner 2007; Ragin 1994).

To ensure validity, the operational measures were based on theoretical constructs developed from the literature on immigrant adaptation and political incorporation, organizational theory, and grassroots organizing. Because the study was exploratory in nature, with the intent of building an organizational explanation of success, the theoretical constructs integrated what is known in these three bodies of scholarship about immigrant political activism, coalitions, and organizational processes for policy change. Furthermore, the questions developed in the interview protocol were intended to allow space for each participant to explain their definition of successful impact and outcomes. This process allowed for patterns to emerge based on pre-determined categories, as well as those that emerged through the interview process. If patterns in the data collected varied from predicted patterns, the analytic framework was adapted accordingly. These strategies ensured the strength of validity and reinforced the explanatory power of the findings.

Limitations of the Research Process
This study centers on examples of how grassroots coalitions — one type of mediating institution — influence state health policy change. At the organizational level, the analysis explains how and why certain factors contributed to coalition building and political capacity for making demands in the policy process. This is one area of immigrant political incorporation in which little empirical research has been done, and in which the research findings make a contribution. However, there are three limitations

to the methodology used, and thus to the findings presented here.

First, in this type of case study, the external conditions present in each case inevitably produce variation. The greater the number of cases, the more conclusions can be drawn about how and why certain factors contribute to outcomes. On one hand, the realistic constraints of time, access, and financial support limited the number of cases included in this particular study. On the other hand, important findings common in both states and across coalition examples emerged, contributing new knowledge to understanding the relationship between mediating institutions and immigrant political incorporation. To strengthen the external validity, more cases should be investigated using the same theoretical propositions, organizational processes, and outcomes (George and Bennett 2005; Yin 2003).

The second limitation is content-specific: the research design did not incorporate an explicit investigation of individuals' leadership development and increased civic participation as a function of the coalitions and their member organizations. While the findings illuminate the kinds of organizational and environmental conditions that lend themselves to successful political action through the grassroots' activity of the mediating organizations, they do not explain whether or not these conditions impact individual political participation, which is also a dimension of political incorporation. The theory developed in this study now provides a new set of propositions from which this investigation can occur.

Finally, I have been both insider and outsider in the research process. My practitioner experience in the field of community organizing has shaped my training as a scholar and my approach to empirical inquiry (Naples 1997). In developing this project, I identified a gap between practitioners' knowledge of the challenges organizations face in mobilizing immigrants for civic and political action and the limited scholarship that investigates organizational factors that impact such efforts. I therefore located a research opportunity that would strengthen both theory and practice.

Following the first set of interviews, I recognized specific ways in which my experience as an organizer influenced my approach to the research, my orientation to the questions, and my methods in the field. This identity as a scholar-practitioner became more apparent during fieldwork in California where gaining access to organizations for interviews with staff and organizers was more difficult. The struggle I faced was not unique to social science researchers (Reinharz 1997). However, I connected this challenge of gaining access to my experience as an organizer—I interpreted this difficulty as further proof of a disconnect between the theory and scholarship of organizing with the realities practitioners face in the field. This, too, informed my approach to data collection and the analysis that followed. It ultimately proved beneficial to the findings of the research.

I learned through the course of data collection that one helpful strategy for gaining access and connecting with respondents was to share with them the origins of the project and more details about my own practitioner experience. As the process of data gathering grew more comfortable, I also became more intentional about sharing general background on the research questions with respondents as a way of contextualizing the inquiry. What initially felt like an awkward introduction to the interviews became a natural, integral dimension of my interview technique specifically because participants had requested this information. This also strengthened the research process, as I was able to develop interview strategies for exploring conceptual ideas through probes that had direct application to an organizer's practice.

In some instances, I knew the individual being interviewed or we knew each other through mutual colleagues. In most cases, especially in Massachusetts, this afforded me access I might not otherwise have had. In situations where I did not have a direct connection to a respondent, I found that I gained credibility once they learned about my background. Participants asked questions such as: "Where did you work?" or "Who did you work with and for?" or "What is your research about and how will it be used?" or "Am I going to be quoted on this?". Often times, I found that sharing my practitioner experience enabled respondents to talk more freely about their own experience and perspective. In so doing, we found a pathway that opened the door to deeper conversations about the dynamics of coalition organizing work.

Being a researcher with "practitioner eyes" enabled me to have a common language with the interview participant. In reflecting on the research process and in reviewing field notes, I found that this led to more trust and candor. This was true in several instances with organizers who directly expressed their skepticism about the interview or scholarship on organizing in general. When my research collaborator was present during interviews in Massachusetts, he also played this role: his expertise, experience, and common connections with a respondent gained us access where I did not have previous relationships.

On the other hand, some may view the insider-outsider relationship as a limitation. LeCompte (1995) describes the research process as an inherently political process, one in which both researcher and participant are actively engaged in a dynamic process of exchange. In this type of social science research, the relationship between interviewer and interviewee is bound to have some impact on the data collected. According to Reinharz (1997), documentation of this interaction is an essential component of fieldwork that leads to stronger research findings (18). Upon reflection of field notes and analytic memos, I found that my orientation as a scholar-practitioner was an asset to the research process. It strengthened the content of the data collected and the process of theory building. That said, to account for my concerns about the impact of an insider-outsider status, I identified during coding and analysis those occasions where information obtained from respondents may or may not have been influenced by the kinds of interactions described above. To further ensure validity, I discussed these instances with colleagues seeking their additional feedback on my initial interpretation of the data. When possible, I also verified facts with other sources.

TABLE 3: Analytic Categories

I: Inter-organizational Development: Coalition Building

1. Mix of organizational types
   - Heterogeneity of constituencies represented
   - Variation in expertise (advocacy, grassroots, policy analysis)
   - Past experience (tactics/strategies/policy area)

2. Public standing/reputation of partner organizations

3. Existing relationships/networks available to take advantage of political opportunity

4. Resources drawn from member organizations
   - Diverse contributions

5. Agreements among partners
   - Contributions to coalition
   - Shared decision making power between partner groups
   - Shared mission: congruous as organizations/ coalition

6. Conveners

7. External funding

8. Existence of multiple coalitions (competition/collaboration)

9. Internal organizational commitments
   - Dedicated staff time
   - Contribution of financial resources
   - "Fit" with strategic priorities

10. Policy threat/opportunity as catalyst for formation

TABLE 3 Cont: Analytic Categories
II: Intra-organizational Development: Internal Capacity Building
1. New skills/resources within individual organizations
• Impact on future strategizing and action plans
• New organizational structures
• Learned skills (ex. Signature campaigns)
• Identify/recruit/develop new leaders
• Internal legitimacy for work
2. Constituent mobilization
• Base building/expanding membership
• Member participation in actions
• Opportunity to educate members
• Leadership development
III: Claims-making
1. Legislative influence
• Policy change (not perception of legislators)
2. Legislative pressure
• Public hearings
• Legislative visits
3. Involvement in policy formulation
• Involvement in implementation planning

CHAPTER FIVE

Massachusetts and California: 2004-2007

Between 2004 and 2007, Massachusetts and California witnessed a growing movement to organize community-based organizations, unions, health consumer groups, and medical and civic associations into coalitions intended to influence legislative action on access to health care.[33] Convening organizations with a proven track record of health care advocacy spearheaded these efforts, and were central to developing mobilization and action strategies for policy change. At the same time, political will for health reform in the Massachusetts and California legislatures was also growing. In Massachusetts, key legislators, including the Speaker of the House, Salvatore DiMasi, stepped up in support of major changes to the state's health care system. Likewise, in California, Governor Schwarzenegger championed a "coverage for all Californians" initiative, beginning in January 2007.

---

[33] Appendix 2 contains a complete list of organizations by coalition, including a list of sponsors and endorsers for the ACT Campaign and the *Yes on Prop 86* ballot initiative. Appendix 3 contains short descriptions of key organizations featured in the case narratives.

77

Access to care for foreign-born residents was not an explicitly stated policy goal in either state. However, if the proposed legislative initiatives passed, one outcome of both state's laws would be changes in immigrant health coverage. Each case represents a distinct policymaking and grassroots organizing environment, and together, they show how statewide coalitions mediated immigrant health interests into state policy change with varying degrees of success. Table 4 provides an overview of coalition members with immigrant constituencies.

MASSACHUSETTS
Overview
Massachusetts has seen a marked increase in its foreign born population in the last twenty years. The U.S. Census' 2008 American Community Survey reports that close to 15 percent of the state's total population is foreign born. It is also estimated that between 2004 and 2007 approximately 300,000-400,000 undocumented immigrants resided in Massachusetts.[34] The growing foreign born population has transformed the demographic composition of many Massachusetts' towns and cities. While traditional immigrant communities in parts of Boston, Fall River and New Bedford, Lowell and Lawrence continue to host new immigrant populations, smaller middle class and predominantly white towns, such as Framingham, Leominster, and Fitchburg, have had more dramatic demographic shifts as immigrants seek better access to affordable housing and employment not readily available in the larger urban core. The current flows of immigration

---

[34] In 2008, it was estimated that this total came closer to 200,000 (Passel 2005; Passel and Cohn 2009).

have elevated the significance of understanding how immigrants adapt and integrate economically, socially and politically in Massachusetts.

Health Policy
Historically, Massachusetts has been generous with public benefits for new immigrants and refugees. The Massachusetts legislature filled the Medicaid gap left from federal welfare reform in 1996 by expanding Mass Health coverage to legal permanent residents who had been in the United States under five years. All children and pregnant women, regardless of immigration status, were eligible for state funded health coverage (Fremstad and Cox 2004). In 2002, Governor Mitt Romney eliminated funds available for Mass Health coverage, and 10,000 immigrants — including 3,000 elderly and disabled — lost access to these state-sponsored Medicaid benefits (Fremstad and Cox 2004). With expansion gains made through health reform in 2006, Mass Health covered all low-income legally residing residents. The state has not extended public benefits to undocumented adults, other than through the Health Safety Net, also known as the "free care pool" for individuals without any other means of health coverage.

Existing organizational infrastructure
Massachusetts is known for its large and densely connected network of non-profits, social service agencies, and advocacy organizations. There is also a long history of civic activism and grassroots organizing across the state. This has been especially true in Eastern Massachusetts, where many organizations have worked together on past legislative and grassroots initiatives. They have established on-going, allied relationships with each other and among

key legislators. This organizational network and its relationships at the legislature have served as a foundation for responding to events in the public policy environment. In the case of health reform, existing organizational conditions made it possible to build a coalition of diverse organizations who each brought to the alliance a different set of resources and skills, a range of constituents, especially across lines of race and class, and a distinct set of relationships among key stakeholder groups. Despite this variety, the groups were able to establish common ground around a set of shared interests and policy objectives.

Background to Campaigns
Between 2004 and 2007, two campaigns impacted policy changes affecting immigrant adults in Massachusetts. The MIRACLE Campaign[35] was formed during the 2004-2005 legislative cycle by a small group of policy and advocacy organizations. The coalition came together in response to the 2002 loss of Medicaid benefits for 10,000 legal permanent residents. With outside funding support, the coalition launched a legislative campaign that resulted in a partial budget victory in June 2005, restoring Medicaid benefits to 3,000 elderly and disabled immigrants.

Around the same time, health care reform organizing in Massachusetts expanded. In 2004, Health Care for All, a statewide advocacy organization, spearheaded a campaign to pass this comprehensive health care reform, convening a group of organizations that formed the "Affordable Care Today!" (ACT) Coalition. Across the state, health care

---

[35] MIRACLE stands for Massachusetts Immigrant Health Restoration Advocacy Campaign for Long-term Equality.

organizers, policy experts, and advocates joined forces to influence what would become major policy reform. On April 12, 2006 a compromise bill was signed into law. This effort involved those organizations active in the MIRACLE Campaign from the outset and incorporated their original policy goal of including all legal residents in the reformed health system. Though multiple health policy goals were at play throughout the ACT Campaign, this investigation focused on those policy goals and organizing objectives related to restoring immigrant health coverage for adults. The following description centers on those coalition members in both campaigns that have immigrants as a main constituent group.

MIRACLE Campaign

To expand coverage for all legal permanent residents, the MIRACLE Campaign was a precursor to the larger ACT Campaign. Six local organizations formed the MIRACLE Coalition in 2004, with funding from The Boston Foundation and the Blue Cross Blue Shield Foundation for planning and implementation. The Public Policy Institute took a lead role in convening five other partner groups: the Massachusetts Immigrant and Refugee Advocacy Coalition (MIRA), SEIU 615's Voice and Future Fund, the Latin American Health Institute, Health Care For All, and the Massachusetts Law Reform Institute. The Coalition's main policy objective was to fully restore access to Mass Health for legally residing immigrants.

The partner groups each had a track record of working either directly or indirectly with local immigrant communities. MIRA and SEIU 615 had the most extensive contact with immigrants or with immigrant advocates and service providers. They provided a strong connection for the coalition with immigrant constituencies most affected by the policy. The campaign also received endorsements from local health clinics that predominantly serve immigrants and their children. The other partner organizations of the MIRACLE Coalition provided both policy and legal expertise. In addition, there was a history of collaboration on past campaigns among many of the partner organizations.

The MIRACLE Coalition accomplished part of its policy objectives in 2004. Governor Romney's legislative veto in June 2004 led to reduced funding available for coverage, as well as restrictive administrative policies[36] for eligible immigrants seeking Mass Health. Throughout the summer, staff and organizers from the MIRACLE Coalition were able to negotiate with legislators to reinstate benefits for approximately 3,000 elderly and disabled immigrants through the budget process. During the 2005-2006 legislative cycle, most partner groups involved in the MIRACLE Coalition joined the statewide health reform initiative in some capacity. Within this larger effort, the MIRACLE Coalition achieved its original policy goals of full restoration of coverage for legally residing immigrants.

---

[36] Sponsor deeming is an administrative provision that holds immigrant sponsors responsible for covering the health expenses of those seniors and disabled persons they have sponsored to come to the U.S. An individual is granted access to Mass Health coverage only once the immigrant seeking care and his or her sponsor proves that they are unable to afford care. With the enactment of Chapter 58 this administrative provision was no longer in effect.

ACT Campaign

Beginning in 2004, Health Care for All, under the direction of John McDonough, convened over thirty organizations to form the ACT Coalition. McDonough had long been an advocate of health reform in Massachusetts, first as a state legislator for thirteen years and now as head of the state's leading consumer health advocacy organization. The diverse organizations involved in the coalition included consumers, patients, community and religious organizations, businesses, labor unions, doctors, hospitals, health plans, and community health centers. The ACT Campaign strategy combined a legislative campaign with a ballot initiative—two simultaneous campaigns with synergistic policy goals. The ACT Coalition was responsible for the legislative campaign, and the MASS ACT Coalition was intended to create outside pressure on the legislature to pass health reform. The ballot initiative campaign served as an alternate action channel should the legislative campaign fail (Thompson 2003).

An eleven-member executive committee governed the ACT Coalition, with a larger steering committee also involved in decision-making. Nine of the organizations in the ACT Coalition led MASS ACT. They coordinated signature gathering for the ballot initiative, as well as other mobilization activities for the legislative campaign. Of the partner organizations in the MIRACLE Coalition, only Health Care for All and SEIU 615 participated in MASS ACT. The other MIRACLE Coalition partners were, however, members of the larger ACT Coalition. Grassroots organizations with large immigrant constituencies also were recruited to the campaign. The Greater Boston Interfaith Organization (GBIO), Neighbor to Neighbor MA, and the Coalition for Social Justice were central to MASS ACT's ballot initiative campaign.

Like the coalition partners involved in the MIRACLE Campaign, the ACT Coalition carried a similar pattern of diverse organizations with distinct expertise and roles. In the MIRACLE Coalition, the ACT Coalition and MASS ACT, early agreements among coalition members solidified their commitment to the campaign goals and the coalition's guiding principles. The core set of guiding principles in the ACT Coalition and MASS ACT shaped the strategies and actions of each group, and was intended to be the foundation on which the members could hold each other accountable. The agreements clarified roles and responsibilities, and established norms for decision making.

The legislative campaign and the ballot initiative ran concurrently from the Fall 2005 through Spring 2006. Members of MASS ACT launched their campaign in the Fall to collect 66,000 signatures of registered voters in order to put a statewide referendum question on the November 2006 ballot. Each of the nine organizational members made a commitment to either collect signatures, contribute financial resources or both. GBIO, Neighbor to Neighbor, the Coalition for Social Justice and SEIU 615 recruited and trained their members to collect signatures. Each organization formulated plans for where to collect signatures, how to delegate volunteers, and what mechanisms would be used for tracking and monitoring their progress. In the Spring, an additional 11,000 signatures were needed, even as the legislature neared passage of the bill. This signature gathering campaign was intended to stand as a credible threat to the legislature if legislation consistent with the coalition's policy goals did not pass.

A decisive juncture for coalition partners in MASS ACT was whether or not to include on the ballot question the expansion of coverage for legal permanent residents. This debate did not surface during the initial drafting of the coalition's proposed legislation. It did, however, catalyze significant discussions early on among MASS ACT partners when internal opinion polling showed that including "immigrants" in the initiative's language would be a liability to the success of the ballot measure among Massachusetts' voters. Through brief, yet critical, internal conversations among members, the coalition remained committed to including immigrant coverage in both the legislative and ballot language.

In April 2006, the legislature approved a compromise bill that, for the most part, reflected the central policy goals and guiding principles of the ACT Coalition and MASS ACT. On April 12, 2006, Governor Mitt Romney signed "Chapter 58" into law, instituting one of the most sweeping state health reforms in the nation (Belluck and Zezima 2006). The provisions of this new law improved access to affordable health insurance for the uninsured and working poor, instituted an employer assessment fee for those companies that do not provide health insurance, and expanded Medicaid coverage for some of the state's poorest residents, including legally residing immigrants. This accomplished the central aims of the original MIRACLE Campaign goals.

Following the passage of Chapter 58, MASS ACT's Ballot Campaign came to an end. While the ballot initiative never went to a November 2006 vote, the signature campaign was used throughout the legislative process to educate and engage a grassroots force that was often mobilized to action. GBIO, Neighbor to Neighbor, the Coalition for Social Justice, and SEIU 615 mobilized their membership base not only during the signature campaign, but also for public actions at the State House. Delegations of members met with legislators, filled hearing rooms, attended and spoke at press conferences, and applied bottom-up, grassroots pressure on legislators to make policy decisions that reflected their interests and those of their members. In *Lessons Learned to Date from the Massachusetts HealthCare Reform*, Wcislo, et al., (2007) note that the "broad coalition of organizations working on reform was critical in providing a louder and more strategic voice than any one group could develop on its own" (37). This proved to be one of the most significant results that organizers pointed to as a result of their participation in the ACT Coalition.

Moving Ahead

As policy implementation took effect in 2007, the ACT Coalition entered a new phase of action. It remained committed to ensuring the implementation of health reform based on its guiding principles of fair, affordable, and accessible health care. Affordability of available insurance plans for low-income residents was of primary concern for coalition members as was the needed outreach and education among low-income residents about the stipulations of the new law. Building and sustaining a broad base of grassroots support continued to be a central component of their strategy for achieving these implementation goals. Health Care for All hired additional staff to coordinate the campaign, and several grassroots and community groups continued to be active members in the coalition's strategy and action. An organizer from SEIU 1199 now serves on the Commonwealth Health Insurance Connector Authority Board, the implementing body for the new health policy.

In the implementation phase, GBIO spearheaded an education and outreach campaign to target low-income residents about resources for accessing health coverage under the new law. GBIO also conducted a health care affordability study among its members to determine reasonable rates of insurance plans for their constituents.[37] From seventy workshops conducted in over fifty congregations and community institutions, GBIO collected survey data (N=589) that was then analyzed in response to rates being set by the Connector Board. MIRA has also worked with its member organizations, especially immigrant health providers, community health centers, and social service agencies, to support outreach and enrollment among low-income immigrants in the new Commonwealth Care program and health safety net programs.

By 2008, only 2.6 percent of Massachusetts' residents were uninsured, the lowest percentage in the nation (Long, Cook, and Stockley 2009). As with most states, however, Massachusetts was also hard hit by the recession that began in 2007, increasing the challenges for successful implementation of Chapter 58 (Goodnough 2009a). Budget projections in 2009 anticipated major cuts in public programs, including a reduction in funding for the health safety net and subsidies for low-income health insurance

---

[37] The results of this study are recorded in *Mandating Health Care Insurance: What is Truly Affordable for Massachusetts Families?* (Greater Boston Interfaith Organization 2007).

coverage. To reduce the growing deficit, a July 2009 state budget proposal eliminated funding for coverage of over 30,000 legal permanent residents who qualified under the Massachusetts plan for Commonwealth Care but were ineligible for federal Medicaid because of the five-year bar. While the proposed cut would have saved the State $130 million, the cost impact would have been felt elsewhere — particularly by hospitals that care for the poor and by individuals who would have to pay higher amounts for co-payments and prescriptions (Goodnough 2009a, b). Among those organizations that pressured the governor and the legislature for the restoration of coverage were Health Care for All, MIRA, and the Massachusetts Hospital Association. By September, partial funding of $40 million had been negotiated, providing minimal health coverage for immigrants who have been in the U.S. less than five years. While this was yet another limited success for immigrant advocates, the struggle to provide health coverage to low-income immigrants goes on. This population remains one of the most vulnerable in the state, as it continues to be subject to the constant changes in available state funding, affordability rates set by the Connector Board, and health policy decisions made by the legislature.

CALIFORNIA

Overview
Like Massachusetts, access to health care in California has been an ongoing concern that reached new levels of public debate after 1996. Estimates of California's uninsured population range between 19 and 24 percent: in 2008, 5.5 million adults (24.5 percent) under age 65 and 1.1 million

children (11 percent) were uninsured.[38] The scope of California's population makes its health care policy arena distinct from all other states.[39] Most of the state's uninsured are citizens and documented non-citizens (Brown, Pourat, and Wallace 2007). Despite expansion of children's coverage through State Children's Health Insurance Program (SCHIP) and the state and county level enrollment programs, California ranks 36th in the nation for children's coverage (Brown, Pourat, and Wallace 2007; Kaiser 2008). The undocumented in California—the largest and most vulnerable population in the state—remain dramatically at risk without access to even basic care. However, they make up a small proportion of the State's total uninsured population. According to a study conducted by UCLA's Center for Health Policy Research, approximately 136,000 undocumented children and 1 million undocumented adults do not have access to care (Brown, Pourat, and Wallace 2007).

The public, non-profit and private sectors have taken important steps in responding to California's health care crisis, yet most agree that the lack of coverage, access, and quality of care continue to be significant public health problems that warrant government intervention (Fremstad and Cox 2004; Hoffman 2003; Capps et al. 2005; Reardon, Anderson, Capps, and Fix 2002). Where state and federal

---

[38] See Kaiser 2008 statehealthfacts.org. Also see analysis of Current Population Survey, March 2007 Supplement conducted by Paul Fronstin, Employee Benefit Research Institute and published by the California HealthCare Foundation.

[39] See Reyes (2001) for comprehensive overview of California's population differences and disparities in wellbeing based on socioeconomic status, race, and ethnicity.

policies have fallen short, many of California's fifty-eight counties have collaborated with community-based health providers and non-profit social service agencies to pick up the slack for health coverage to the uninsured, regardless of status. This network of county agencies and local organizations has lead the way in providing care to the uninsured and under-insured of California, especially the state's foreign born. However, it has remained insufficient and many groups have pressed for more state involvement and increased public spending on care.

Similar to Massachusetts, the description that follows examines statewide coalition organizing that occurred between 2004 and 2007 in response to legislative health policy changes that would affect immigrants. Its primary focus was on the legislative activity and grassroots organizing to provide statewide health insurance coverage to undocumented children. This example also captures coalition activity that followed Governor Schwarzenegger's January 2007 announcement of health reform as it related to coverage for undocumented children.

Health Policy
California is one of twenty-two states that provide state-funded coverage to immigrants. Like Massachusetts, it has been historically liberal in providing access to public benefits for poor immigrants who were barred from federal Medicaid after 1996. At that time, California established eligibility criteria to cover all legally residing immigrants through both MediCal and Healthy Families. Most children are covered under these state programs or through county-level programs set up to provide coverage for immigrant children, especially the undocumented who

are ineligible for state coverage. In 2000, five of fifty-eight counties provided subsidized coverage to undocumented children and adults, and an additional twenty-seven counties were planning and implementing similar programs with a mix of county dollars and private funding support during the time period studied (Hirota et al. 2006). In addition, pregnant women regardless of status have pre-natal coverage through the state's Healthy Families program.

This level of coverage remained consistent after 1996, despite various threats to cuts in funding. There have been moderate successes at the state and county level for increased funding for clinics and enrollment programs. Local coalitions of public, private and non-profit organizations have been at the forefront of these organizing efforts. Especially in the area of children's health, advancements have been made. Children's Health Initiatives exist in twenty-nine of the fifty-eight counties, and have been one vehicle for increasing enrollment and coverage for poor children, regardless of status (Stevens, Cousineau, and Rice 2006). Santa Clara County's policy decisions and program implementation of children's health coverage provided an important precursor to larger statewide efforts at children's health reform (Trenholm et al. 2007). With at least half of California's counties providing some level of health coverage to children, political pressure has grown to implement state-level policy that provides universal access to care for children, regardless of status.

Existing Organizational Infrastructure
Because legally residing children and adults have had coverage through state and federal programs, organizing

for immigrant health policy change in California primarily focused on improving language access statewide, increasing enrollment and outreach services for existing public programs, maintaining budget allocations for state-funded programs, and expanding access to care for the undocumented. The broad networks of advocates and community organizing groups throughout the state have tackled various components of these immigrant related health policies.

When Governor Schwarzenegger was new to office in January 2003, he proposed to eliminate state replacement programs for immigrant public benefits. The state's leading immigrant organizations, including the then California Welfare Collaborative, convened a formal coalition, and generated rapid-fire action in response to the Governor's threat. Organizations that had a statewide presence and reputation at the legislature combined their expertise with the grassroots power of community-based organizations. They involved multiple kinds of organizations in local and statewide actions that pressured legislators and ultimately influenced the Governor to change his position. By the time of the budget revision in May, Governor Schwarzenegger dropped his effort to slash public benefits programs for immigrants. The 2003 mobilization was an important success among immigrant organizations. This victory, coupled with the already existing progressive state policy supporting immigrant health, are integral to the historical context in which groups in California attempted to organize for coverage expansion for the undocumented.

Three additional factors contribute to the context of the 2004-2007 campaigns to impact health policy change for undocumented children. First, initiatives aimed at comprehensive health coverage such as that found in Santa Clara County provided a model for effective public policy centered around local collaboration and integration of services.[40] The progress made statewide by social service and health providers, community organizations, and local government has ensured greater county-level coverage through the Children's Health Initiatives. Second, other advocacy and organizing groups looked to these models for best practices that could be implemented as statewide coverage options for all children. Third, California health foundations, including the California Endowment and the California Wellness Foundation, proactively focused their funding priorities on health care access, particularly following the tobacco settlements of the 1990s.[41] They have identified and recruited organizations that they believe have the power, resources, and political leverage to engage in health policy campaigns. They also have provided

---

[40] Mathematica Policy Research, Inc., the Urban Institute, and the University of California, San Francisco conducted a study of Children's Health Initiatives in three counties and found significant improvements in child well-being as a result of increased access to and quality of care (Trenholm et al. 2007). The study was funded by the Packard Foundation.

[41] As energy around health reform has grown at the state and national level, health care foundations have convened diverse stakeholders to strategize how best to build momentum for more sustainable policy change. The Blue Cross Blue Shield Foundations in several states, The Robert Wood Johnson Foundation and the Henry J. Kaiser Family Foundation have collaborated with policy experts and practitioners in conducting research, funding initiatives, and communicating usable information about best practices for health policy change.

necessary funding for local and statewide coalitions organizing around specific issues like health disparities and access.

Background to Campaigns
Californians for Healthy Kids
The 100% Campaign was funded and convened by the California Endowment to pool the resources of the state's three leading children's advocacy groups—Children Now, The Children's Defense Fund of California, and the Children's Partnership. Since the mid-1990s, these organizations have worked to expand statewide coverage and enrollment for children in California. Their main policy objective is to pass legislation that will guarantee comprehensive access to coverage, including for undocumented children. The 100% Campaign initially focused on incremental policy change that would improve rates of insurance and enrollment among California's children. Over time, the campaign shifted its focus to statewide, universal coverage.

To further a statewide policy agenda, the California Endowment facilitated a partnership in 2002 between the 100% Campaign and the Pacific Institute of Community Organizing of California (PICO CA), a statewide congregation-based organization. PICO CA added grassroots strength to the effort for universal children's coverage. The organization brought with it a large constituency of families directly affected by the issue, a commitment to covering undocumented children, and political muscle and experience organizing around health concerns. Together, the 100% Campaign and PICO CA made up the Californians for Healthy Kids (CHK) Coalition.

PICO CA began its statewide policy work in 1993, with a focus on education and health care. Nineteen affiliate organizations make up the PICO CA federation in California. Many affiliates are embedded within immigrant communities, including those in the Bay area, Los Angeles, San Diego, and the rural communities of the Central Valley. Locally-based, grassroots organizing in each affiliate is the main vehicle by which decisions are made about the overall policy direction for the statewide organization. PICO CA's interest in organizing for health policy change emerged as local affiliates throughout California began to identify health care access as a priority issue for its membership. PICO CA affiliates had been achieving local wins aimed at improving access and increasing county-level children's health enrollment. These local wins, such as the victory in Santa Clara County, catalyzed the organization's campaigns for statewide coverage.[42]

The three children's organizations brought to the coalition comparable expertise in children's policy advocacy. While they each contributed similar resources to the coalition, there was variation in legislative and political know-how, policy analysis skills, and media savvy based on the experiences of the organizations' leadership. All four organizational partners in the CHK Coalition had experience with past campaigns for children's health, and over the life of the partnership, developed enhanced skills and effectiveness for advocacy and organizing for statewide policy change. The political

---

[42] See Wood (2002), Chapter Two for discussion of the history of PICO CA statewide organizing and the relationship between local organizing and statewide policy influence.

power of the organizations' leaders was also essential at the legislature. Throughout the CHK Coalition's campaigns, one or several of the organizational leaders were able to leverage relationships in the Assembly that moved their agenda forward.

None of the organizations in the CHK Coalition specifically identified as an immigrant organization, yet PICO CA has broad and deep roots in California's communities of color. These relationships across the state connected the CHK Coalition's policy work directly to the interests and needs of immigrants. Since its formation, the CHK Coalition had varying degrees of success in achieving its policy goals. During this same time period, California's immigrant advocacy organizations worked to ensure that immigrants continued to receive adequate access to the state-funded replacement programs. For the most part, they were successful in maintaining this coverage through policy advocacy campaigns like the 2003 effort against Governor Schwarzenegger's proposed elimination. While they were informally allies, members of the CHK Coalition and the immigrant advocacy organizations had never been formally aligned in a coalition for policy change.

PICO CA and the 100% Campaign organized as an alliance through several strategies: coalition building, legislative advocacy, a signature campaign and ballot initiative, and grassroots' voter mobilization. The CHK Coalition was launched during the 2004-2005 legislative cycle, when they first attempted to pass legislation that would ensure universal coverage for all children. In April 2005, the Coalition organized a children's health insurance rally in Sacramento. Over 4,000 people traveled to the capitol to meet with legislative leadership about their policy priorities. This event engaged and energized much of PICO CA's constituency. Local leadership in PICO CA was relied on for the coordination and turnout of members from across the state. The presence of and public commitments made by key legislative and administration leaders, including Kim Belshé, Director of Health and Human Services, the Senate President, and the Head of the Assembly, indicated support for the passage of the legislation. This event had internal significance to the Coalition because of the momentum gained from a statewide mobilization. The public commitments made by decision-makers also gave the coalition external significance. The California Assembly passed this legislation the following summer. However, despite promises given, Governor Schwarzenegger vetoed the legislation, citing fiscal concerns and an inadequate funding mechanism for the new policy.

Having had such positive results throughout the course of the campaign, this failed policy outcome angered and disappointed CHK Coalition partners. Almost immediately, the Coalition launched its next campaign during the summer of 2005 — to put children's coverage on the ballot through an initiative process. This campaign came to be known as the "Yes on Prop 86" Campaign. Collaborating with the American Cancer Society and the California Primary Care Association (CPCA),[43] the Coalition investigated possible initiatives for the November 2006 ballot that would by-pass the legislature and go directly to voters. With uncertainty in the state budget and little to no support among Republican

---

[43] CPCA is the association that represents non-profit community clinics and health centers.

legislators for a tax, they believed this strategy would be winnable because of its clear funding mechanism.

During the same time, the California Hospital Association also developed an initiative campaign for a cigarette tax increase, positioned to be on the June 2006 ballot. The Hospital Association had the financial resources to accelerate the initiative process, and was able to collect and submit the necessary signatures quickly with paid signature gatherers. Children's coverage organizers believed that if the Hospital Association's initiative went to the June ballot and won, the California electorate would be less likely to vote for another cigarette tax a few months later. Given that, the groups negotiated a partnership and agreed to a November 2006 ballot initiative with a $2.60 tax to fund multiple health measures, including coverage for undocumented children.

The Yes on Prop 86 Campaign was the product of a series of negotiations in December 2005 between the Hospital Association, the American Cancer Society, the American Lung Association, the American Heart Association, CPCA, PICO CA, Children Now and the Children's Partnership. Without authorization from the national office to participate in the initiative, the Children's Defense Fund of California stepped out of involvement during this phase of action for children's coverage. Likewise, the California Endowment withdrew from its convening role, as legal limitations restricted the Foundation's involvement in this kind of political action.

The eight main organizational partners coordinated the Yes on Prop 86 Campaign, each bringing with them their original political consultants. Individual organizations devoted part of their staff time to the Yes on Prop 86 Campaign. With financial contributions from coalition members, the campaign also hired staff, placing four organizers regionally across the state to coordinate signature gathering and get-out-the-vote efforts.

In order to qualify the Initiative for the ballot, the partner groups had to collect over one million signatures. Of this total, the volunteer signature gathering campaign activities were significant for the CHK Coalition partners, especially PICO CA. PICO CA and the American Cancer Society relied on local leadership and their extensive membership bases throughout California to collect signatures entirely with volunteer power. One PICO affiliate alone collected over 12,000 signatures. According to one PICO organizer, the organization gained "street cred" through this work, and increased their visibility both locally and statewide—a resource they will be able to leverage in the future. In total, the American Cancer Society and PICO CA collected over 175,000 signatures through their networks of members and volunteers.

PICO CA, Children Now, and The Children's Partnership also continued their legislative efforts during the Yes on Prop 86 Campaign to expand funds for county clinics and monies available to target enrollment of eligible uninsured residents. Here, they had moderate success. On September 19, 2006, Governor Schwarzenegger signed into law SB 437 aimed at improving enrollment in and retention of health insurance through California's Medi-Cal and Healthy Families programs. It was estimated that this policy change would increase enrollment of an additional 94,000 children.

Even though immigrant coverage was a central dimension of the policy objectives in the Yes on Prop 86 Campaign, immigrant organizations were peripherally involved in organizing and advocacy activities. Over the

Fall 2006, additional community organizations and groups signed on as endorsers to the campaign, though their involvement in planning and coordination was limited. Among these endorsers were immigrant organizations that assisted with get-out-the-vote efforts and provided guidance on media relations. For example, Latino Coalition for a Healthy California led "Latinos for 86" during the get-out-the-vote phase of the campaign. The California Immigrant Policy Center also worked with the partners in the CHK Coalition to develop more effective messaging about undocumented coverage. Though these immigrant groups were consulted on certain campaign-related issues, they were not involved in the steering committee's major decision-making.

The Yes on Prop 86 Campaign faced considerable opposition from tobacco companies against the increase in the cigarette tax, so much so that a question surfaced about whether or not the proposition violated the Master Settlement Agreement of 1998. With pressure mounting from the tobacco lobby, staff from the Governor's office and members of the democratic leadership encouraged coalition partners not to file the initiative. The opposition also launched a media campaign against Proposition 86 in August 2006, uncommon timing for November elections. The focus of the opposition's campaign was not, surprisingly, centered on the fact that the initiative would increase coverage for undocumented children. Rather, it focused on the use of taxpayer dollars as the primary funding mechanism instead of allocating state funding for public health measures through the legislative and budget process.

Ultimately, Proposition 86 failed by 280,000 votes, a small margin for a state with an electorate of 22 million people. Several factors contributed to the loss. First, there was low-voter turnout and a relatively uncompetitive race for Governor that year. In polls leading up to the election, Governor Schwarzenegger was far ahead of Democratic opponent, Phil Angelides. With that, those likely "yes" votes for Proposition 86, especially from the democratic base, were not as activated to turnout on Election Day. There was also a significant vote-by-mail effort in which many who cast their ballot early did so without exposure to any media in favor of Proposition 86. The Yes on Prop 86 Campaign began running television advertisements less than two weeks prior to Election Day.

Within the campaign, there were mixed feelings about whether or not the coalition partnership with the Hospital Association negatively impacted their chances of winning on children's coverage. Proposition 86 included a variety of health measures that incorporated the interests of multiple stakeholders. Children's coverage was not the sole policy priority. In addition, the campaign did not publicly talk about those elements of the proposal that would expand access to undocumented children. In the wake of a growing national dialogue about comprehensive immigrant reform, it was challenging to mobilize for expanded coverage, while local immigrant groups were also responding to vicious anti-immigrant attacks at the same time.

Certainly disappointed with the outcome, staff and organizers from coalition partners also believed the campaign had positive effects. It strengthened the capacity of the partner groups to work together. The initial signature gathering effort built up the grassroots resources, especially among PICO CA affiliates galvanized to action because of the shared concern for children's health coverage. The coalition also established new relationships and deepened existing ones among constituents and members, at the legislature, and between organizations, especially the American Cancer Society. These results were considered to be important successes, despite the failure of Proposition 86 at the polls.

Immediately following the defeat, the CHK Coalition launched a new effort to hold the Governor accountable to his 2003 campaign promise to support health coverage for all children. "Fulfill the Pledge" was a short-lived campaign begun in late November 2006 and spearheaded by PICO CA to mobilize its core constituency. The central tactic was to track the governor's public statements during the state-of-the-state address in January 2007 in order to ensure that he made children's coverage a priority for the coming year. When Governor Schwarzenegger's announced health reform in January 2007, the group had to re-strategize this accountability campaign. They continued in their plans for viewing parties and web-based voting on the state-of-the-state address. However, it was clear that they would need to develop a new plan of action for moving forward with children's health coverage.

Comprehensive Health Reform: 2007
With the Governor's announcement of a comprehensive health reform proposal in January 2007, the CHK Coalition maintained their policy focus on universal children's health coverage. Other coalitions for health reform emerged in response to the Governor's plan, but neither the children's advocacy organizations nor PICO CA joined these new coalitions. While they were not formal members, CHK did communicate with other coalitions about legislative strategies and policy developments at the

Capitol, especially on the children's coverage component of health reform.

In addition to the Governor's plan, three additional plans were released in early 2007: one each from the senate and assembly leadership along with a universal coverage proposal from Senator Sheila Kuehl. Each of these plans included some dimension of access to care for undocumented children and adults. Where Republican Governor Schwarzenegger's proposal included plans for covering undocumented children and adults, Democratic Senator Don Perata's original proposal included no coverage for this population.

The policy proposals released in January 2007 prompted many health-related interest groups and other stakeholders to initiate plans for influencing legislative decisions on reform. Of note, two coalitions convened organizational partners from grassroots, community, and health consumer organizations. These coalitions focused on coverage expansion and affordability for adults and children. They developed a variety of political strategies for affecting change, and had varying degrees of legislative influence in this uncertain policy arena. During the 2007 campaign for comprehensive health reform, immigrant organizations were more actively involved in coalition efforts than in those previously organized for universal children's coverage.

The "It's Our Health Care" (IOHC) Campaign was a statewide coalition seeking to pressure the Governor and the legislature to pass comprehensive health reform based on seven main principles (see Appendix 4). The coalition was comprised of a mix of organizations, including health advocacy and consumer organizations, unions, senior citizen groups, and several organizations with large immigrant constituencies. Their main organizing strategy was to build a statewide coalition with regional and local coalitions in key legislative districts. Targeted recruitment of coalition partners began in February 2007.

Health Access, California's leading health consumer group, SEIU and the CA Labor Federation were the convening partners. They each provided considerable financial and staff resources to the campaign. Similar to the Yes on Prop 86 Campaign, the IOHC Coalition hired staff and campaign consultants to coordinate the legislative, field, and media segments of the campaign. Individual organizations, especially those sponsoring the coalition, also designated staff with specific responsibilities to the campaign. Between February and April 2007, IOHC recruited members, developed its policy goals and organizing strategy, hired the campaign staff, and began to mobilize regional coalitions in Los Angeles, the Bay area and San Diego. The campaign employed a variety of organizing tactics, each month focusing on a different tactic for pressuring legislators.

While the IOHC Coalition was forming, three organizations convened the "Having Our Say" (HOS) Coalition: The California Immigrant Policy Center, the California Pan-ethnic Health Network (CPEHN) and the Latino Issues Forum. Rooted in a cross section of California's major ethnic groups, the HOS Coalition concentrated solely on the interests and policy goals of communities of color. CPEHN coordinated the coalition in collaboration with staff from each of the convening partners. A group of organizations that attended early coalition meetings in March and April 2007 developed a set of five guiding principles to which other organizations joining the coalition were asked to sign on to (see Appendix 4).

The HOS principles directly related to the interests of communities of color, with an explicit goal of affordable, quality care for all residents of California, regardless of status. The Coalition's main objective was to influence legislative decisions based on the policy positions they developed from these principles by engaging coalition partners in action strategies for change. They intended to be a voice for the coalition's priorities within the larger health reform organizing efforts. A secondary objective was to build their collective capacity, especially with smaller organizations, for state policy action.

The HOS Coalition developed independently of the IOHC campaign. There was, however, organizational overlap in membership between the two coalitions. Several organizations participating in the HOS Coalition were also members within the IOHC Coalition, including the HOS convening partners. Each coalition had statewide reach. While the policy objectives and organizing strategies of both Coalitions were similar, the HOS Coalition was explicit in its commitment to ensuring coverage for undocumented children and adults.

Three reasons catalyzed the HOS Coalition to form. One precipitating event was the lack of coverage for undocumented children or adults in Senate President Don Perata's initial proposal. Without coverage for a large proportion of the State's uninsured, this proposal raised concerns among advocates because the Senate leader—a Democrat and ostensibly an ally to the cause—had put forth a plan that appeared to be more conservative than the Governor's. Second, while a main priority of the IOHC Coalition was universal coverage, immigrants and people of color were not the primary focus. For this reason, the HOS convening partners felt it important to concentrate on policy goals related specifically to these constituent groups.

Third, forming the HOS Coalition became an occasion to build new organizational networks and to influence public policy specifically based on the interests of their constituents. HOS was the first formal partnership between the convening partners. Though the details of the Coalition's "bottom line" policy positions were developed over time, their common concern of accessible, quality care for communities of color united the group and guided their decisions. HOS was a vehicle to connect beyond an immigrant-only focus, but not so broadly that the coalition's interests were subsumed by the IOHC Campaign that represented more expansive health priorities. The coalition's conveners also believed they could benefit from organizing separately. Based on their experiences in past campaigns, they wanted to establish an up-front presence in the policymaking process. They also wanted to engage new organizations never before involved in this type of state-level legislative activity. Coalition formation was, therefore, an opportunity to connect similar kinds of organizations across the state, many of which are small and had no prior presence at the legislature.

Moving Ahead

The policy environment in 2007 was ripe with opportunity to make policy gains, a fact that organizers and advocates readily acknowledged as significant about this moment in the history of state health reform. Throughout 2007, the CHK Coalition continued its legislative advocacy and grassroots' work to expand access to the currently 763,000 uninsured children. It worked with legislators to sponsor different pieces of children's health legislation in the Spring 2007.[44] The children's advocacy organizations were involved in drafting this legislation and in testifying at hearings on behalf of the coalition's interests. PICO CA affiliates held local health forums across the state. They continued to mobilize members through community action meetings and legislative visits. These sessions were aimed at holding targeted legislators accountable for covering all children and for finding an adequate funding mechanism to do so. They also lobbied for the inclusion of a tobacco tax comparable to that proposed in Proposition 86.

Into the Fall 2007, the IOHC Coalition and the HOS Coalition pursued similar grassroots and advocacy strategies to influence legislative decisions about the proposed reforms. Organizations across the state mobilized to have an impact, and devoted their financial and people power resources to the effort. Tracking the multiple legislative options and educating members about their potential impact was a large component of their work. Internally, the coalitions and their member organizations evaluated the various proposals for adherence to their core principles and "bottom lines." The

---

[44] For example, the goals of AB 1 and SB 32 legislation were to: 1) Extend Medi-Cal and Healthy Families eligibility to children in families below 300% federal poverty; 2) develop affordable insurance options for children in families with incomes above 300% of poverty; 3) simplify enrollment and renewal process with an aim towards access and retention; and 4) create smooth transition for children in local CHI's to statewide insurance programs.

IOHC and HOS coalitions each attempted to make visible the need for comprehensive health care reform through media coverage and storytelling. They lobbied legislators and organized local and regional events to target lawmakers. When feasible, HOS Coalition members participated in IOHC sponsored events such as press conferences and legislative visits.

As the effort to pass health reform unfolded, questions emerged about the viability of the proposed plans and the political feasibility of their passage in the California legislature. Legislative activity through the Fall 2007 reflected this uncertainty, as the Governor's office, legislators, and health advocates attempted to develop a plan for comprehensive reform that met the interests of multiple stakeholders and contained what policymakers believed would be practical and effective financing mechanisms.

On December 17, 2007, the California Assembly passed AB x1-1, *The California Health Security and Cost Reduction Act* (sponsored by Assembly Speaker Núñez). A companion initiative was filed on December 28, 2007 and set for the November 2008 ballot. This Initiative was designed to provide the necessary funding to support AB x1-1, once approved by the Senate and signed into law. By January 2008, AB x1-1 had moved to the Senate Health Committee.

Advocates and organizers from all three coalitions mobilized their base to lobby members of the Senate Health Committee throughout the month of January. Internally, the coalitions and their member organizations assessed whether or not they could support AB x1-1 either as it stood or amended if it did not contain measures that met the criteria developed in their initial principles. By mid-January, different members of the IOHC and HOS Coalitions took public positions on AB x1-1 outside the context of the coalitions. Ultimately, pressure from the Governor's office, external interest groups, and supportive legislators was not enough to propel AB x1-1 through committee. Without the support of Senate President pro Tem Perata and the committee's chairwoman, Senator Sheila Kuehl, the bill was held in committee on January 28, 2008.

The failure of California's health reform in 2007-2008 left the future of children's coverage uncertain. Despite this failed attempt, gains were made in the years that followed in the fight for statewide coverage of California's undocumented children. PICO CA continued organizing in conjunction with the national mobilization in support of the reauthorization of the federal Children's Health Insurance Program that passed in February 2009. Together with the children's advocacy organizations of the 100% Campaign, PICO CA has also continued to develop local and state action strategies for increasing enrollment and access to coverage for all children as well as moving ahead on national health reform. Individual members of the IOHC and HOS Coalitions embarked on mobilization strategies for federal health reform in 2009. They also were active in advocacy campaigns in the wake of California's budget crisis that threatened heath access programs across the state. Finally, the HOS Coalition secured funding to continue building its capacity as a coalition and organizing community-of-color organizations for state-level political action.

TABLE 4: Coalition Matrix of Related Organizations	
Coalition	**Examples of Organizational Members with Immigrant Constituencies***
MIRACLE Coalition	• *Convened by the Public Policy Institute* • Latin American Health Institute • Health Care for All • Massachusetts Immigrant and Refugee Advocacy Coalition • The Massachusetts Law Reform Institute • SEIU 615's Voice and Future Fund
ACT Coalition/ MASS ACT	• *Convened by Health Care for All* • Coalition for Social Justice • Greater Boston Interfaith Organization • Massachusetts Immigrant and Refugee Advocacy Coalition • Neighbor to Neighbor MA • SEIU 1199 • SEIU 615
Californians for Healthy Kids Coalition	• *Convened by California Endowment* • PICO CA • 100% Campaign:[45] Children Now, the Children's Partnership, and the Children's Defense Fund of CA

---

[45] None of the organizations in the 100% Campaign have direct ties to immigrants, yet they do represent immigrants in that their work is focused on access to care for all of California's children.

TABLE 4 Cont.: Coalition Matrix of Related Organizations	
Coalition	Examples of Organizational Members with Immigrant Constituencies*
Having Our Say Coalition	• *Convened by California Pan-Ethnic Health Network, Latino Issues Forum, and California Immigrant Policy Center* • Asian Pacific American Legal Center • Bay Area Immigrant Rights Coalition • The California Partnership • Coalition for Humane Immigrant Rights of Los Angeles • Korean Resource Center • Latino Coalition for a Health CA • National Immigration Law Center • National Health Law Program
It's Our Health Care Coalition**	• *Convened by Health Access* • Asian and Pacific Islander American Health Forum • Asian Health Services • California Immigrant Policy Center • The California Labor Federation • California Pan-Ethnic Health Network • The California Partnership • Korean Resource Center • Latino Coalition for a Health California • Latino Issues Forum • SEIU

See Appendix 2 for complete list of organizations by coalition.
**Noted organizations are those that overlap with the HOS Coalition*

CHAPTER SIX

Organizational Analysis: Process and Outcomes

OVERVIEW

The Massachusetts and California cases present two approaches to statewide coalition building for public policy change. Neither example studied was explicitly intended to build immigrant power per se. Rather, immigrant interests were part of larger campaigns for health policy change. In this process, immigrant health interests were preserved through inter-organizational partnerships and intra-organizational development, despite variable policy outcomes in the two states. Eight inter-organizational factors contributed to coalition strength and cohesion, and three intra-organizational factors made a difference in building up the political capacity of individual partner organizations. Though the claims-making process yielded different kinds of success, the interests of immigrants would not have been integrated into the policy arena had it not been for this form of coalition organizing. Therefore, these findings are both structural and process-oriented. Table 5, found at the end of this chapter, summarizes the findings from the cross-case analysis.

The analysis examined political power and capacity outside the typical forums of immigrant organizing for public action.   The main stakeholder groups, the organizational mix, and the health policy goals of both organizing efforts crossed race, ethnicity, and class. As a result, the findings speak to broader issues of immigrant political incorporation into "mainstream" politics. Lessons about coalition form and behavior are applicable to other settings—not only in statewide campaigns for policy change, but also across different forms of organizing for public influence.

That said, the examples are not devoid of the contexts in which they occurred. The social and economic forces of each state shaped the operating environment of the coalitions.   Context is also an ongoing phenomenon, determined by cycles of action and reaction. Coalition viability was highly influenced by past political events and organizational dynamics unique to Massachusetts and California. These factors reflect the history of each state's political institutions, as well as the organizational outcomes and political dynamics of earlier campaigns for policy change. These dimensions also influenced how and why the coalitions formed. They affected which partner organizations joined the coalitions, what strategies for action were chosen, how the groups coordinated activities and made decisions, and the extent to which they achieved success. Therefore, the findings are specific to the individual examples and their context of political action, as well as generalizable to a set of theoretical ideas common to both about inter-organizational partnerships, internal capacity building, and claims-making success.

At first glance, inter- and intra-organizational dynamics explain how and why the coalitions were able to make health policy demands. Where this theoretical formulation holds true, it is also true that each set of dynamics can be interpreted as outcomes of the campaigns in and of themselves. Common factors contributed to inter-organizational strength, led to greater political capacity, and affected the policy outcomes. Inter-organizational strength was central to coalition cohesion and sustainability over time. Likewise, building internal capacity — the skills, resources, experience, and relationships needed for statewide action — through intra-organizational development was integral to their ability to exert public influence. The coalitions employed similar political action strategies, and both the inter- and intra-organizational dynamics affected the coalitions' ability to win policy gains. Furthermore, the successes of each coalition have not been without challenges. With diverse organizational actors, each coalition also illustrates potential barriers to coordination and effectiveness as well as threats to success that can come from within a coalition and from the operating environment.

In Massachusetts, a broad coalition was successful in the context of dense networks with a high degree of inter-organizational connection among the players. The main organizational actors were diverse, yet complementary, and were brought together in one coalition to respond to a specific health policy problem. They had a shared mission and common set of goals that under girded their formation as a coalition and held them together. Though they faced various threats to achieving their goals throughout the campaign, this type of coalition building and public action yielded successful policy change.

California illustrates a different story of success where multiple coalitions existed within the same policy arena.

The Californians for Healthy Kids (CHK) Coalition had only moderate success at winning policy gains between 2004 and 2007. By the end of January 2008, the legislature failed to pass comprehensive health reform, and the coalitions studied did not achieve their goals. Despite unsuccessful policy change, there were other kinds of success. Like Massachusetts, the main partners in each coalition were drawn from dense networks in response to particular health policy problems, of which coverage for undocumented children was one. Complementary resources and skills existed among organizational partners that were beneficial to accomplishing policy goals. These goals, and the action strategies used by the coalitions to accomplish them, often overlapped. While there was limited inter-organizational cohesion *across* the coalitions, some gains were made in advancing the interests of immigrants through the processes of coalition building and internal organizational development.

COALITION BUILDING THROUGH INTER-ORGANIZATIONAL PARTNERSHIPS

Coalition building was the main vehicle by which inter-organizational strength developed within the campaigns. The examples provide evidence of eight factors that facilitated robust partnerships, contributed to coalition effectiveness, and that can be replicable in future campaigns: existing relationships, conveners, external funding investments, steering committees with early agreements, internal commitments, reputation and public standing, heterogeneity, and shared mission. Organizational partners added resources and different expertise to the overall strength of the coalitions. The relationships between coalition partners—those that existed prior to the campaigns and those that evolved over the course of the campaigns—enabled the organizations to take advantage of political opportunities in the policy environment, and to navigate potential external threats to cohesion and sustainability. In both states, the time was right for the organizing initiatives and each coalition developed inter-organizational power integral to its capacity for influencing legislative change in this context.

Existing relationships
The dense organizational networks of non-profit, advocacy, and grassroots organizations in both states laid the foundation for responding to the political opportunities present in the policy environment. They made it possible for organizations to respond to the interests and needs of their main constituent groups, specifically because there was a previous organizational infrastructure that could be mobilized for action. These relationships enabled the coalitions to take advantage of opportunities they might not otherwise have been able to as individual organizations. In both states, not all partners had experience working together but most had some overlapping, prior relationships, especially among organizations that acted as conveners. Existing relationships were the basis on which coalitions formed. It was a process that was catalyzed in large part by convening organizations that operated as the hub of these relational connections. At different times in their campaigns, they accessed these relationships in service to accomplishing campaign goals. Additionally, many organizers explained that by partnering with other organizations they were able to accumulate greater power to impact statewide issues. They believed that by acting

together they had greater credibility and political leverage than if they acted as stand-alone organizations.

For many reasons, the time was right for each campaign: there was substantial support for health policy reform within the state legislatures as well as a strong network of potential coalition partners willing to organize for common policy change goals. In Massachusetts, this was a selling point for several partner groups recruited to join the campaign. For some organizations, participating in the ACT Coalition and MASS ACT was an opportunity to translate policy commitments into winnable action. For others, it was an opportunity to build internal capacity by mobilizing their constituency around an issue that directly affected their members. For the CHK Coalition there was a common rationale for joining together in the Yes on Prop 86 Campaign. Despite the success at the legislature in 2005, the Governor's veto propelled the CHK Coalition to develop an immediate strategy for pushing their agenda forward. They built on existing relationships and new partnerships to form the Yes on Prop 86 Campaign because they believed it was a winnable strategy. The relationships with the American Cancer Society, the American Heart Association, the American Lung Association and the California Primary Care Association proved advantageous in the coalition's negotiations with the hospitals because of the broader constituent base they represented as a group. These relationships were also valuable in their continued pressure on the legislature and Governor despite defeat during the health reform battle.

Conveners
Conveners had a prominent role in all the coalitions investigated. They recruited partner groups, developed the

campaign strategy, leveraged financial resources, and facilitated decisions with other coalition leaders. Across all the campaigns, leaders gave careful consideration to the partners they recruited to the coalition. In Massachusetts, Health Care for All, convened the ACT Coalition and MASS ACT, identifying those organizations they believed would enhance political viability. They recruited a wide mix of sponsors and endorsers, with a purposeful eye towards those organizations that would contribute to the coalition's strength, especially given the likelihood that external pressure on the legislature could make a difference in the law.

This was also true in California. The California Endowment was at the center of the partnership for children's health coverage, convening the CHK Coalition with these goals in mind. They wanted to develop a unified voice for children's health coverage with a group of players who had political credibility on the issue and the organizational capacity for advancing a policy agenda. The steering committee of the Yes on Prop 86 Campaign also considered political viability. They targeted organizations to sponsor and endorse the campaign that would lend credibility, resources, and the political heft needed for a winning strategy. This resulted in the combined power of sponsoring organizations that represented a range of constituencies: children, hospitals, clinics and primary care professionals, nurses, and the cancer, heart and lung associations. Like Massachusetts' ACT Campaign, the Yes on Prop 86 Campaign generated public support from hundreds of elected officials, civic and community organizations, and professional and business associations. This mix was not always beneficial to the campaign's cohesion. Proposition 86 included multiple health measures including children's health coverage. The range of health policy goals, along with the diversity of organizations involved, was a potential source of tension and threat to cohesion among coalition partners.

The It's Our Health Care (IOHC) Coalition resembled the Massachusetts' ACT Coalition, though it was much larger in scope. Like Health Care for All, Health Access convened a diverse coalition in collaboration with the unions to influence the legislative outcome of health reform. They emphasized the need for a coalition that represented multiple constituencies, and targeted organizations with that in mind. IOHC coordinated its campaign in similar ways to a ballot initiative campaign, gathering support from many stakeholders, each representing a different constituent group, policy concern, or health interest. Guided by Health Access, the anchor organizations of the IOHC steering committee represented this mix, and included the AARP, the SEIU State Council, the California Labor Federation, and a cross-section of grassroots, immigrant, and ethnic-based community organizations.

The Having Our Say (HOS) Coalition emerged as an organizational response to previous experiences on the margins of larger coalitions. Its policy goals were consistent with the IOHC Coalition. However, the conveners wanted to articulate a set of priorities rooted in the needs of their primary constituents, not bundled together with other stakeholder groups. By convening a separate coalition, the HOS Coalition represented the shared health interests of communities of color, including coverage for undocumented children and adults. This decision reveals a different coalition building strategy than in Massachusetts. In addition to being allied with the heterogeneous group of IOHC coalition partners, the HOS Coalition chose to have a distinct voice on the issues directly affecting their constituents, and a separate strategy for political action out of those specific priorities.

External funding investments
Similar to conveners, external funding helped to initiate the campaigns and sustained their work over time. Private foundations made considerable investments in the coalitions and campaigns, often supporting part or full-time staff to coordinate campaign activities. Organizers in Massachusetts reported that this support indicated confidence in their track record, as well as a commitment on the part of funders to the policy goals of health coverage for immigrants (in the MIRACLE Campaign) and the expansion of health insurance (in the ACT Campaign). With its activist orientation, the California Endowment catalyzed the formation of the initial 100% Campaign, then recruited PICO CA to strengthen the political and grassroots capacity of the CHK Coalition. It maintained an on-going relationship with the organizations in order to facilitate the coalition's effectiveness. The California Endowment also provided funding to the HOS Coalition in its early stages of formation. This financial support, geared towards capacity building, made it possible to provide mini-grants to small organizations new to statewide coalition work. The MIRACLE Coalition received funding from the Blue Cross Blue Shield Foundation that served a similar purpose: to support the work of individual coalition members in service to the goals of the whole coalition.

During the Yes on Prop 86 Campaign, members of the steering committee, like the California Hospital

Association and the American Cancer Society, made substantial financial commitments to the campaign. Without these contributions, the coalition would have lacked the necessary resources for sustainability, especially because they could not rely on money from private funders during a ballot initiative campaign. These resources also supported the media campaign needed to counteract the considerable opposition.   In the ACT Coalition as well as in IOHC's Campaign, union members made similar financial investments, either directly to the campaign, or indirectly through the designation of their staff to the coalition's work. As expected, these kinds of investments increased organizational commitment to the campaign, and added to long-term inter-organizational power. It also increased the power of certain groups in the steering committees.

Steering committees with early agreements
Initial agreements made between partnering organizations were an intentional and strategic component of each coalition's creation. These initial agreements varied from formal ones facilitated by conveners or granting organizations to informal, "off the record" conversations about how partner groups would communicate, what resources they would contribute, and how decisions would be made about strategy and action. The agreements enabled each partner to clarify their roles and responsibilities in the coalition.   From the outset, they established norms of communication and participation among members of the coalition steering committees. The effectiveness of this mechanism varied throughout the campaigns, depending on how well articulated and, at the same time, how flexible the agreements were. These

agreements were noted as a core element of coalition cohesion and a tool for accountability. Organizers emphasized that shared decision-making power among coalition leadership was essential, if at times, a very difficult process to navigate.

Agreements developed in the MIRACLE Coalition guided the responsibilities of the partner organizations, though there was some fluidity because of the small number of players. Perhaps because the ACT Coalition was broader and more diverse, clear, formal agreements played a more prominent role in organizing the coalition. Organizers in MASS ACT reported that those early agreements established ground rules for how decisions would be made, who had authority and responsibility to make those decisions and provide input, and how accountability among coalition partners would be structured. These early agreements, and the coalition's shared understanding of those agreements, were essential during intense discussions and decision-making.

The California Endowment's on-going role in the CHK Coalition ensured that the organizations held to their established agreements, readjusting them as needed. Organizers reported that trust has grown over time among the leadership of the CHK Coalition. They consult one another not only on coalition strategy, but also on their internal strategies that may be related to campaign goals or activities. The funding support and involvement of the foundation contributed to sustaining the coalition's cohesion throughout its various campaigns.

Finally, while at first the HOS Coalition developed informally among the three conveners, there were also clear structures in place from the beginning that reinforced cohesion throughout this coalition's first campaign. The group recruited over thirty organizations. Once they committed to a set of core principles and shared agreements, regular in-person and conference call meetings promoted greater communication and accountability among the partnering organizations. As the coalition moved into its next phase of action following the 2007 campaign, these initial agreements and principles served as a foundation from which they built capacity, developed strategies for organizing, and made decisions.

Internal commitments
When organizations agreed to participate in a coalition they made an internal organizational commitment. These commitments contributed to overall effectiveness in that coalition strength hinged upon the individual contributions made by anchor organizations. In some cases, organizations dedicated staff time specifically to the campaigns. Here again, the convening organizations acted as coordinators, bearing significant responsibility for regularly bringing organizers and staff together, and serving as hubs for information, communication, strategizing, and decision-making. As noted above, convener organizations also contributed financial resources to the coalition, especially among executive or steering committee members of the ACT and MASS ACT Coalitions, the Yes on Prop 86 Campaign, and the IOHC and HOS Coalitions. The health consumer organizations and the labor unions in both states invested sizable staff and financial resources in the campaigns.

While integral to the strength and sustainability of the coalitions, staff and financial commitments were enhanced by the commitment of people power from grassroots organizations. The Greater Boston Interfaith Organization

(GBIO), Neighbor to Neighbor MA, the Coalition for Social Justice, and PICO CA's affiliates were an integral resource to the coalitions because they committed their constituent base to the campaigns' political action strategies. Each of the nineteen PICO affiliates made different commitments of time, internal leadership, and volunteers to the signature gathering and Get-Out-the-Vote activities for the Yes on Prop 86 Campaign. GBIO, Neighbor to Neighbor MA, and the Coalition for Social Justice consistently mobilized their memberships for signature gathering, legislative hearings, and press conferences. Most concretely, the commitment of these organizations is reflected in two metrics: the number of signatures gathered by each organization and their turnout totals at legislative events. Less concretely, but equally important, was the commitment the leadership made to working internally to build legitimacy among members, educate them, and create opportunities that increased their responsibility for and involvement in campaign activities over time.

The sustainability of the CHK Coalition—despite its losses—provides a good example of how internal commitments made by member organizations are crucial to coalition viability. Children's health coverage was a long-term priority for each member organization, and through this shared mission, organizations committed to the coalition's work. But shared vision for change alone cannot sustain a coalition, especially when an effort fails. Each organization had dedicated staff time to the effort. In certain instances, this was determined and supported by a grant agreement. In others, the partner organizations decided to devote additional resources to the work, as was evident in the Yes on Prop 86 Campaign.

For PICO CA, certain affiliates that did not receive funds directly from the California Endowment devoted significant amounts of time, energy, and resources to collecting signatures. This commitment grew out of their desire to have a direct impact on an issue that mattered to their members. Some of the affiliates that were involved extensively saw the campaign as an opportunity to build their local organizing infrastructure. Similarly, GBIO identified the ACT Campaign as a mechanism by which they could grow their political capacity to a new level, and develop leaders to have a statewide impact. In the implementation phase, the ACT Coalition continued to build on these internal commitments to advance the coalition's work, which also advanced GBIO's success in strengthening its organization internally.

Reputation & public standing
Reputation and the public standing of individuals and organizations alike contributed to the inter-organizational strength of the coalitions. The experience and credibility of individual leaders was a primary reason given for why organizations decided to join and stay involved in a coalition. This dimension positively affected each coalition's ability to leverage important legislative relationships, funding from outside sources, and community support. In Massachusetts and California, the reputation that existed among many partnering organizations formed the basis of coalition relationships. The early agreements fostered accountability. Confidence in each other's reputation and potential contributions to the campaign enhanced an initial degree of trust. It also catalyzed interdependence over time and increased the shared need to resolve internal disagreements as they

surfaced. Acting together and having successes along the way facilitated greater trust among the partners.

The organizational members of the MIRACLE and ACT Coalitions had an established reputation for their values, positions on issues, and strategies for political action. Each was looked to as a resource that could contribute something unique to the campaign effort. From this, their credibility as a coalition was built up through the life of the campaign. Like the MIRACLE and ACT Coalitions, partner organizations in the CHK Coalition had a reputation for their progressive position on children's health issues, the quality of their work, and the political and legislative capacity to carry forward a policy agenda. PICO CA's past successes on children's health, its political sophistication, and its grassroots capacity added strength to the overall partnership when they joined the CHK coalition in 2002. These dimensions of public standing contributed to the overall political capacity of a coalition, and lent it external and internal credibility throughout the various campaigns.

It is important to note that organizational reputation and public standing is not devoid of individual personality and charisma. Inevitably, leaders will facilitate or inhibit the reputation an organization holds amongst its collaborators and allies. Though this factor was not explicitly explored during the interviews, many respondents commented on the powerful (and in most cases, positive) impact that individual leaders had on the credibility of the coalitions in the policymaking process. For example, members of the clergy played a central public role in Massachusetts' health care campaign and during events organized by PICO CA. As official leaders of religious institutions, their moral authority was identified frequently in the press and among organizers as an element of legitimacy that lay leaders did not necessarily have in the campaigns.   Likewise, in each campaign, experienced leaders with a specific policy expertise or track record in legislative action played crucial roles in leveraging support and moving the policy agendas forward.

Heterogeneity

Conveners drew upon a range of potential allies from the tightly networked advocacy and organizing communities in Massachusetts and California.   Targeting a mix of coalition partners was a key strategy conveners used to bring together the right blend of resources, political clout, and power for effectively influencing policy change. Heterogeneity — the diverse resources from a mix of policy, advocacy, and grassroots organizing groups — added strength to the coalitions.   This heterogeneity was a common feature in all of the statewide coalitions.   The MIRACLE Coalition, the ACT and MASS ACT Coalitions, and the IOHC Coalition had a balance of policy advocacy and grassroots-oriented organizations. The CHK and HOS Coalitions had a similarly balanced mix of organizational type, but maintained a more homogeneous combination of their priority constituencies.   For the CHK Coalition, the focus was entirely on children; for the HOS Coalition, it was communities of color.

The heterogeneity of expertise, resources, and constituency proved advantageous, especially in Massachusetts. Coalition members complemented each other's contributions.   Some partner organizations had experience and a positive reputation for successful legislative campaigns.   Other coalition members brought unique policy and lobbying expertise. Others (sometimes the same member) brought public standing as policy experts or as representatives and leaders of key constituencies including labor, immigrants, and the faith community. Within the heterogeneous mix of the coalitions, unlikely allies also came together to execute the campaigns. Several groups involved in the ACT Coalitions, the Yes on Prop 86 Campaign, and the IOHC Coalition had been historically on opposite sides of the bargaining table. An example from both states is the coalition relationships between labor unions, hospitals, and the business community. One union organizer commented that they do not often sit around the same table with the business community as collaborators.

In both states, the constituencies of the grassroots organizations were affected directly by a lack of adequate health coverage. They gave local roots to statewide coalition work. This was a particularly important asset for the groups in California given the state's size and scope. PICO CA in the CHK Coalition, the unions in the IOHC Coalition, and the ethnic-based, community organizations in the HOS Coalition were links to a broad base of communities from which people could be mobilized. Similarly, GBIO, Neighbor to Neighbor MA, the Coalition for Social Justice and SEIU connected to different low and middle-income communities across Massachusetts, many of whom would benefit from coverage expansion.

The participation of unions and the grassroots organizations in the MASS ACT Coalition provided, among other assets, the ground troops for gathering signatures and filling hearing rooms. This was also true in California's Yes on Prop 86 Campaign where PICO CA affiliates and the American Cancer Society mobilized their base of volunteer members to execute a significant portion of the ballot campaign with unpaid signature gatherers. PICO CA had, until then, been building an infrastructure of affiliate member organizations willing to engage in statewide action that was then activated for the signature campaign. Among the health care reform coalitions in California, grassroots connections were important to their strategy of organizing regional coalitions, and for mobilizing legislative pressure at local district offices and in Sacramento. However, these relationships were not as strong among the health reform coalitions as they were in the ACT and CHK Coalitions. Following the 2007 campaign, the HOS Coalition identified strengthening grassroots relationships as one of its strategic goals for the next phase of organizing and action.

Lastly, heterogeneity provided flexibility of response during the campaigns. While heterogeneity intrinsically carries a potential threat to cohesion, the prior existence of overlapping networks of trust and cooperation played a major role in managing internal stresses to coalition unity. Clear agreements about "bottom lines" among coalition partners also helped coalitions sustain themselves through conflict. In the cases of the MIRACLE, ACT and CHK Coalitions, heterogeneity proved essential for maintaining the alliances.

The ACT Coalition provides a useful example of this factor. Some partners had strong expertise in health care and wide-ranging skills in lobbying and advocacy; others had little proficiency in health care policy, but strong political experience in other fields; yet others had extensive track records in successful grassroots organizing. Aligning a legislative and ballot campaign into a coordinated effort emphasized the mutually supportive nature of different skills, organizational types, and constituent bases. These not only strengthened the coalition, but also increased its interdependency. The most striking example of this was a decision by one member to forgo a grassroots mobilization effort planned prior to coalition formation. It decided that replicating a capacity already available among its partners was not a cost effective or politically viable strategy. Rather, the member invested instead in its own area of expertise, expanding its staff to benefit the larger coalition's work. This is a particularly clear example of the interdependence found between inter- and intra-organizational developments in demand making strategies.

CHALLENGES TO INTER-ORGANIZATIONAL PARTNERSHIPS

Two examples from the cases highlight the kinds of inter-organizational challenges that coalitions face in sustaining their cohesion and strength throughout the life of a campaign. These examples are drawn from two analytic categories that emerged as significant in the analysis of coalition building. Almost all respondents discussed these issues in their interviews. In the Massachusetts, shared mission was *the* issue discussed when focusing on issues related to immigrant coverage; in California, multiple coalitions was described as one of the main challenges they faced in organizing in the state. Thus, they are presented here as illustrations of how the coalitions negotiated internal threats to coalition viability.

Massachusetts: Shared mission

The centrality of commitment to a shared mission cannot be overestimated, and is illustrated powerfully in the

Massachusetts case. While each organization in the MIRACLE and ACT Coalitions had a specific motivation for participating, organizational self-interest alone did not drive their involvement. Almost all the groups involved had some commitment to health care reform, even if they did not have related experience. The players in the ACT Coalition came together around a shared set of goals and showed, at a minimum, a willingness to take risks *as a coalition* to accomplish those goals. This shared goal was around health care reform. However, the focus on immigrant health coverage also revealed the importance of a shared mission in coalition building.

The debate about including coverage for legally residing, non-citizen immigrants on the same basis as citizens was not very controversial in the legislation, but was in the language of the ballot question. Following a series of focus groups that showed negative public response to coverage for legal permanent residents, members of the coalition raised concerns about including this policy goal in the ballot initiative that would go directly to voters. Among the coalition partners, there was never a question about whether or not it was appropriate to include documented, non-citizens in the expansion of Mass Health. The question focused on whether or not it would be a viable, winnable issue. Some partners felt that including it would weaken the possible threat of the ballot as pressure on the legislature. Others believed eliminating it would compromise the interests of their constituents, members, and allies.

Among the organizers interviewed there was some debate as to the significance of this moment in the campaign. All respondents, however, confirmed that the decision to preserve the language was rooted in a moral commitment to immigrant health coverage, and an unwillingness to back down from that commitment even if it meant the ballot would fail. It was also during this point in the campaign that members of the MIRACLE Coalition seemed to make a difference within the ACT Coalition. The reputation of those organizations involved in both coalitions, and their ability to leverage internal support, made it possible to preserve immigrant coverage in the ballot and maintain it as a component of the overall policy goals.

Similar to the importance of heterogeneity, the insistence on maintaining the core mission and the unity of the coalition in the face of risks reflected an inter-organizational strategy that depended on the complementary, interdependent roles of the organizational members. The role of grassroots organizations and the members of the MIRACLE Coalition were, in this instance, to be the voice for immigrant health coverage. It is important to note, too, that while the ACT Coalition strongly advocated for the expansion of immigrant coverage, they chose not to attempt passage of coverage for the undocumented as those in California did.

California: Multiple coalitions
Unlike the Massachusetts case where there was one unified coalition, the activity in California around health reform illustrates the inter-organizational dynamics when multiple statewide coalitions work on the same issue.[46]

---

[46] In California, I began investigating the strategies used by the CHK Coalition to pass universal child health coverage and the extent to which they achieved success using those strategies. During the research process, additional coalitions working for

Initially, the CHK Coalition had varying degrees of legislative success towards universal children's health coverage. Following the defeat of Proposition 86, the Governor's health reform proposal in January 2007 shifted the political and organizational landscape in which this coalition attempted to change public policy. Political will increased among legislators, motivated by the executive's strong interest in moving ahead on health reform. Public interest and pressure for expanding children's coverage had also increased over the years, which made it more likely that the coalition could achieve their policy goals in the 2006-2007 cycle. Finally, the IOHC and HOS Coalitions emerged, each focusing some dimension of their action strategy on health coverage for undocumented children. None of the CHK partner organizations joined either of these coalitions, though they maintained allied relationships with members of the other coalitions.

Hundreds of state and local organizations participated in the IOHC or HOS Coalitions. Some organizations were

---

some of the same policy goals formed. The final phase of research, therefore, included the addition of interviews and secondary data analysis of these coalitions. For the purpose of the analysis, I considered three central stakeholder groups involved in the case: the children's organizations; immigrant organizations; and health consumer organizations. Each group of organizations represents the interests of a primary constituency, with their policy goals and priorities flowing out of their constituency's needs and interests. A fourth group of stakeholder organizations are those that either cut across constituency groups or serve as "connectors." By and large, there was significant overlap among organizations in the California campaigns.

members of both coalitions, but played different roles. For example, while the conveners of the HOS Coalition were members of the IOHC Coalition, they were not necessarily leading partner organizations. HOS was a separate coalition, and, at the same time, an important part of the IOHC Campaign because of the constituency they represented. As allies, their reach within community-based organizations in communities of color was an asset to the work of both the IOHC and CHK Coalitions.

Organizational overlap such as this presents a potentially divisive threat, with so many political actors seeking a common policy change in the same arena. Under such circumstances, each coalition's effort is a fine balance between collaborating with allies and competing for the time, resources, and energy of the involved organizations and volunteers. Because there were multiple coalitions with a high degree of cross over, there were also multiple priorities. Each coalition had a set of principles from which they drew their policy priorities, with some match across the coalitions. Where these priorities were not shared, it was possible that different strategies would be used to meet coalition goals, and that these strategies might be at cross-purposes. Support for individual mandate versus single-payer plans was one such example that illustrates where the greatest threat to cohesion occurs. Is it possible to have claims-making success if multiple actors advocate at the legislature and organize the grassroots for essentially the same overlapping goals?

The emergence of the HOS Coalition led to what is perhaps the most central finding from the California example.[47]   Among organizations in California dedicated to health care policy change, there was a disconnect between health policy and immigrant rights advocates. In particular, organizers in both immigrant- and non-immigrant based organizations described a lack of integration between the coalition organizing aimed at coverage expansion for the undocumented and the involvement of immigrant rights groups in those efforts. In the CHK Coalition, this dynamic was not merely about having a voice, or being a key decision maker in a coalition. This dilemma revolved around a shared struggle between immigrant- and non-immigrant based organizations alike about how best to be allies, recognizing that they each have a stake in the policy outcome.

Immigrant organizations expressed frustration that "mainstream" organizations did not see them as a resource for policy strategy or public responses to concerns about health coverage for the undocumented. Likewise, mainstream organizations expressed uncertainty about how best to work across organizations. It is possible that this dynamic was the result of a difference in organizational structure and staffing, especially the racial and socio-economic make-up of those organizations. For example, prior to the Governor's announcement of health

---

[47] This finding is consistent with findings from Ramakrishnan and Viramontes (2006) who distinguish mainstream organizations—those that primarily serve and are staffed by U.S. born whites, versus ethnic organizations that serve and are staffed by immigrants, and other racial and ethnic groups (31). See Chapter 3 of Ramakrishnan and Viramontes (2006) as well as Chapter 2 of Ramakrishnan and Bloemraad (2008) for further discussion.

reform in January 2007 and during the campaigns for children's coverage, California's leading immigrant organizations were not formal members of the CHK partnership. However, they clearly had a stake in the success of that effort. The California Endowment again played a critical role, and attempted to facilitate a stronger relationship among the organizations. By supporting training sessions on public communications about immigrant issues, the Endowment provided a specific opportunity and an intentional mechanism by which the organizations could work together, educate one another, and be a resource for each other in a way that they had not been before.

The distinction made in the interviews between "mainstream" and "immigrant" organizations surfaced as a core inter-organizational challenge. It raised the question of whether or not an advocacy coalition is more likely to win policy gains if it is viewed as more conventional or neutral by legislators and the public. On the other hand, the emergence of the HOS Coalition as a separate coalition addressing similar policy goals raised the question about whether or not the organizational composition of the CHK Coalition was the most effective vehicle by which immigrant interests could be brought into this particular policy arena. While the CHK Coalition advocated consistently for policy change that would directly affect undocumented families, it did not have a *direct* connection to those organizations whose explicit purpose is to represent immigrant interests. This reality may have impeded their ability to communicate effectively on immigrant-related policy problems, given the increasingly hostile political environment. Nonetheless, PICO CA's grassroots' reach into communities of color and immigrant communities gave the CHK Coalition an important level of credibility on this issue, especially because of its past victories on children's health coverage that increased access for undocumented children at the county level.

INTERNAL CAPACITY THROUGH INTRA-ORGANIZATIONAL DEVELOPMENT

Intra-organizational development in partner organizations during the campaigns complemented the inter-organizational strength of the coalitions. Three dimensions of intra-organizational development were found to be integral to coalition power: individual organizations acquired new skills and resources, mobilized their constituencies and engaged new strategies for political action, taking risks they might not otherwise take if acting alone. The outcome of this internal capacity building and growth for several organizations was, in and of itself, a kind of success that can impact future action. As a result of the campaigns, several organizations enhanced their political skills and policy expertise for statewide action, involved new and more members in civic participation, and built internal legitimacy for their organizing initiatives.

New skills & resources

The extent to which an organization invested internal resources reflected different degrees of ownership and buy-in to the campaign goals. This investment was based on several factors. Chief among them was the availability of staff and people power resources. Availability of resources was coupled with a willingness to commit such resources to a statewide organizing project. The extent to which organizations felt they had a stake in the organizing issue appeared to motivate a greater commitment of organizational resources. This internal commitment then benefited the overall coalition's strength. The opportunity to translate organizational mission into actionable steps for policy change also motivated organizations to commit their resources to the campaigns. Participation in statewide coalitions gave them tangible opportunities to influence the policy decisions that would directly affect them and their constituents. Their commitments to a campaign reinforced organizational priorities and values. In this way, participation in statewide campaigns had intra-organizational benefits to the individual organizations and inter-organizational benefits to the coalition: organizational involvement led to new internal skills and stronger relationships with members or clients. New and stronger relationships also developed with other organizations with whom they united around a common policy agenda.

The most significant evidence supporting this finding was among the grassroots organizations. Signature gathering was an example of how involvement in statewide campaigns developed intra-organizational capacity for these organizations. Through these efforts, more and more members were exposed to statewide work. Individuals involved made a commitment to tasks that were tied directly to state health policy change. Participants knew that such changes would impact not only residents in their local communities, but also residents across the state. This was critical: for individuals who had never been involved beyond local organizing campaigns, this activity may have been their first experience making connections to public issues much

larger than in their local areas.   Attending legislative
meetings and hearings for the first time was also an
opportunity to connect the work of their organizations to a
statewide policy arena.

PICO CA, GBIO, Neighbor to Neighbor, and the
Coalition for Social Justice were able to grow internal
political capacity through the Yes on Prop 86 signature
campaign and the MASS ACT ballot initiative respectively.
Active members acquired new skills for a specific kind of
public action, became educated on complex health policy
issues, and developed greater understanding for how their
local organizing work could connect with statewide policy
change. Especially in GBIO and PICO CA, organizers
talked about the new leadership that emerged in the
campaigns. Individual members of the organizations who
had not been involved actively in the past participated in
the signature campaigns. Rather than "just attend
meetings," they participated in action steps from which
they saw direct outcomes.   The grassroots organizations
identified and recruited new members to participate in
these activities, building their own base of volunteers for
future campaigns. For example, even though the question
in Massachusetts never went to the ballot, signature
gathering was a mechanism by which they could mobilize
their base for direct action on an issue that would have
tangible consequences for members and their families.
Interestingly, no group that was interviewed reported
disappointment among members regarding the decision
not to put the issue on the ballot. The connection between
their signature campaign and the successful legislation
was universally appreciated and made the ballot effort be
seen as a success even without a vote.

As a result of these types of activities, participants and staff members alike began to see greater connections to the possibilities of collective power at the state level. Similar conclusions can be made about mobilizations in Boston and Sacramento. In PICO CA, the experience of planning, coordinating, and turning out over 4,000 people connected the membership base in the affiliate organizations to PICO CA's statewide policy work. Like the signature campaign, it equipped organizers with new skills for large-scale political action. For both staff and PICO members, the commitments made by public officials signified that their local organizing could have an impact on statewide policy. Grassroots and union organizers in Massachusetts also described new skills and resources within their organizations that resulted from their participation in the ACT Coalition and MASS ACT. Like PICO CA staff, they learned to execute massive signature gathering, public education, and on-going turnout for public hearings. Several noted that the successes of the campaign helped to build legitimacy for their organization's work among its members, and now provides an opportunity to go back to their base for future action. Participation in the Connector Board (the implementing body of Chapter 58), along with a grassroots outreach to local communities about enrollment, are two ways individual organizations built on their skills from the ACT Campaign.

The extent to which statewide organizing benefited smaller, local organizations was another dimension of intra-organizational development found in California. In a state as large as California, organizers noted the need to connect local work to statewide policy decisions. Having influence matters to these organizations, yet many lack skills and political know-how, or have not been connected to opportunities for public action. Some organizations are more equipped with the skills needed for such statewide policy work. Others need more intensive training and support. The HOS Coalition's recruitment and involvement of small, grassroots groups and service providers made it possible to connect to new kinds of state policy work. The state-level policy advocacy organizations also had an opportunity to connect more directly with grassroots organizations. One organizer involved in both the IOHC and HOS Coalitions described their participation in health reform as an opportunity to learn more specifically how best to work with local community-based organizations on the issue of health care, and how to provide useful support, materials, and resources for organizing and advocacy. This sentiment was echoed among a number of organizers.

Constituent mobilization

Constituent mobilization was a critical aspect of organizational development. Each campaign at some point depended on a group of coalition partners for the mobilization of grassroots power. This was the central activity in MASS ACT, had been an on-going strategy for the CHK Coalition, and was used to generate pressure for comprehensive health reform in California. Grassroots mobilization was also a key mechanism for demand making at the legislatures in so far as attendance at hearings, rallies, and press conferences demonstrated that the coalitions had a public constituency. Mobilization is a strategic opportunity for internal capacity building: by organizing volunteers, leaders, and staff for public action, organizations build up their own resources. It gives organizers a way of connecting the day-to-day activities of organizing with a larger vision for change among their constituents and volunteers, many of whom can directly benefit from legislative victories. The campaigns allowed organizations to demonstrate to members and constituents their own efficacy in a new way. Locally, this happened through public actions like signature gathering, town hall meetings on health care, and local legislative visits. At the state level, the coalitions organized constituents to conduct legislative visits and meet with policymakers, make presentations at public hearings, and participate in large rallies. These actions were a vehicle by which individuals exerted power, made possible by the organizing infrastructure that had been built through the coalitions.

New strategies for political action
Two additional findings emerged as relevant for broad-based, Alinsky-style organizations involved in coalition building. First, broad-based community organizations described coalition organizing for state policy change as a new strategy in which they could achieve their goals. In order to make policy gains and see a direct impact on the lives of their members they have had to engage in both statewide work as well as coalition organizing. Lead organizers from these groups also played an active leadership role in the legislative activity of the campaigns. Their degree of participation at the coalition table was noted as unique, given their common organizing practices where individual members of the organization—not paid staff—tend to lead negotiations with public officials. This was true for both PICO CA and GBIO. To a lesser extent, the same issue emerged with the labor unions and other grassroots organizations, where professional staff or lobbyists tend to take on advocacy roles in legislative

campaigns. Moreover, leadership decisions at the coalition level in both cases were predominantly made by staff and organizers — not by members or constituents. An important question for future research emerges from these findings: to what extent are the political capacity and claims-making outcomes impacted when staff versus individual constituents of an organization interface with legislators and their staff?

CLAIMS-MAKING SUCCESS

Each of the coalitions in Massachusetts and California had varying degrees of public influence through their campaigns. The MIRACLE and ACT Coalitions in Massachusetts saw significant legislative victory through health reform passed in 2006. By January 2008, neither the CHK Coalition nor the health reform coalitions had achieved their policy objectives. Presence at the legislature through public hearings and lobbying visits, their involvement in policy formation, and input into policy implementation were examples of how the coalitions in Massachusetts and California also achieved claims-making success. Though there were similar forms of coalition building, the results of the campaigns differed. We learn here that even though there was variable success in changing public policy, other dimensions of claims-making also contributed to the success of the coalitions. These include legislative influence and involvement in policy formation and implementation.

Legislative influence & involvement in the policymaking process

In making demands on the state legislature, there were constant trade-offs about when to increase pressure publicly versus focusing on direct deliberation and negotiation with decision-makers. Debates about claims-making strategies and tactics were inevitable in heterogeneous coalitions with different skills, constituencies, and political power. The strategy of a combined legislative campaign with a ballot initiative in Massachusetts is one example. Mutual dependency, shared mission, and pre-existing institutional and personal relationships all acted to resolve disagreement about tactical choices without endangering the coalition. The overlap between the coalition's power and its ability to influence the legislative process reveals how the capacity of the coalition grew, and how integral the mix of organizations was to the overall success of the campaign strategy to accomplish its claims-making goals.

In the time period studied, the CHK Coalition did not achieve its claims-making goals. However, in spite of the Governor's veto in 2005 and the loss of Proposition 86, the partners experienced other dimensions of claims-making success. First, the campaign did have some clear legislative victories. Though vetoed by the governor, the 2005 legislation passed in both the Senate and Assembly. In addition, the campaign saw policy change in September 2006 when SB 437 was signed into law. The coalition also had success in applying continuous pressure at the legislature about children's health coverage: their relationships with legislators were strong with a clear sense of who supported and opposed their policy goals. They had regular communication with legislative staff to know what was going on and why. Organizers believed their credibility at the legislature grew over time, and was due, in part, to the fact that they "kept showing up." Finally, the coalition amassed enough influence that they were invited to consult on policies and proposals with legislative staff and the Governor's office. While they did not achieve their ultimate policy goals between 2004 and 2007, the CHK Coalition laid a necessary foundation rooted in credibility and public standing that is evidence of their agenda-setting influence. The HOS Coalition had similar kinds of success, and built positive, on-going relationships with legislators that continue to be a part of their coalition strategy.

LIMITATIONS OF COALITION BUILDING: OPPORTUNITIES & CHALLENGES OF UNDOCUMENTED COVERAGE

In both Massachusetts and California, respondents acknowledged that coverage for the undocumented was *the* most politically potent issue within conversations about immigrant health care. Organizers and staff echoed a common theme that this was an un-discussable issue. Many articulated the need for extreme sensitivity and vigilance when dealing with these policy-related issues so as not to jeopardize even the limited care that the undocumented are able to access.

While the ACT Coalition did not tackle coverage for the undocumented in their campaign, there were particular dimensions of their work that helped to preserve access to care, much of which happened behind the scenes. Organizers who had solid relationships with legislative staff and the implementing body of health reform were able to ensure that emergency care remained available to immigrants without status. They also were able to navigate the complexities of reporting and documentation when an individual seeks care. These actions were critical first steps in creating access to care for this population.

The study of health coverage for undocumented children in California presented a different set of circumstances, especially because of the state's high concentration of foreign-born residents and its undocumented population. California's network of social service providers focused on minority health, advocacy organizations, and politically powerful labor unions shape a multi-layered organizational infrastructure that is attempting to influence the legislative process. Constituent groups, policy goals, and strategies for action regularly overlap among these organizations. Many organizations have worked together in the past, collaborating on local, regional, and state campaigns for increased access to care, improved quality, and better programs. The statewide campaigns for coverage of undocumented children illustrate that multiple challenges exist within a political context of opportunity.

With limited resources, organizations have to make choices about what priorities to invest in. By and large, immigrant organizations and their allies have had to prioritize public action centered on immigration reform. Federal discussions of immigration policy reform have influenced the choices made by these organizations. Across the country, immigrant groups are on the defensive. They have had to react to workplace immigration raids, attempts at restrictive state policies limiting access to public benefits, and proposed anti-immigrant policies at the city and county level, such as verification ordinances.

In California, organizers raised this as a contextual factor that affected their ability (or inability) to focus on issues related to health care between 2004 and 2007. This was true of both statewide and local organizations, including several PICO affiliates. It was not only the immigrant-based organizations that felt pulled by the urgency of responding to anti-immigrant attitudes and policies. Participation in the marches and rallies of the Spring 2006 varied from organization to organization: certain organizations took lead roles in coordinating and planning for these events. In some cases, significant organizational resources were invested in these efforts, often diverting attention away from other organizational priorities in service to mobilizing their base for turnout at rallies, responding to anti-immigrant backlash, and addressing the media. This was certainly true for the immigrant rights groups, some union locals, and churches with large immigrant memberships.

In addition to these contextual factors, immigrant groups faced particular challenges within the larger coalition structure for statewide policy change. The CHK Campaigns for universal children's health coverage built significant momentum statewide as more and more counties successfully implemented new programs for coverage and enrollment. Coverage for undocumented children was one policy goal of Proposition 86, yet it was not central to the campaign's priorities, nor were immigrant organizations involved in the early planning stages. While immigrant groups were allied with this coalition effort, they were not central actors.

The campaign's public messaging was never directly about the expansion of coverage for undocumented children. In fact, the CHK Coalition downplayed the undocumented coverage dimension. They believed it would be the most winnable and politically viable approach to influencing the perceptions of legislators and the public. This approach was echoed among organizers interviewed in Massachusetts as well as those interviewed during the formation of the health reform coalitions in California. In the Yes on Prop 86 Campaign, the focus was, instead, on a reduction in tobacco consumption through the proposed tax. Moving the initiative through a larger coalition with heterogeneous interests was an opportunity for political cover on this controversial issue. In this regard, the two groups had different goals. The lead partner organizations were first and foremost concerned about winning Proposition 86, a tobacco tax to fund many health measures. The immigrant groups, as endorsers, were also concerned with avoiding attacks on immigrants, especially in the wake of serious Republican backlash the previous summer as a children's coverage expansion proposal was attempted in the budget process.

In this instance the peripheral involvement of immigrant-specific groups enabled them to have some influence in the process. Latino Coalition for a Healthy CA spearheaded an effort in support of Proposition 86, and there were other informal relationships with additional immigrant and community of color organizations during the final phase of the Yes on Prop 86 Campaign. With these allies, the CHK Coalition remained dedicated to ensuring that all children were covered under the initiative. Yet, from the start, there was an imbalance of power among the groups. In any campaign this is bound to occur, especially when different partners are contributing more resources than others. However, the relationship between these allies was also strained as described previously. It was unclear how and to what extent the immigrant groups would be involved in the campaign, especially in how best to communicate publicly about coverage for undocumented children. The core tension existed in whether or not they would need to prepare for potential anti-immigrant attacks if surfaced by the opposition, and if so, how they would respond.

Four factors point to what makes collaboration difficult for these kinds of allied organizations. First, the organizations have varying expertise on the policies at play. Limited knowledge of facts, data, and experience with potentially sensitive public issues might impede an organization's ability to communicate effectively on the issue at hand. Whether or not a group has a direct connection to this issue is another possible explanation for miscommunication and an inability to coordinate with others on a response. The salience of undocumented coverage is at the forefront of this dilemma. The children's organizations, though sympathetic to the concerns of immigrants, did not explicitly represent their interests. They had a different motivation for being involved in the policy arena than the immigrant groups, and this, in and of itself, may have also been a source of tension.

Third, the nature of the relationships that existed between the children's campaign organizations and PICO CA is different than those with the immigrant organizations. Between the children's groups and PICO CA, there was a formalized relationship and, consequently, greater alignment. This was the primary relationship in which they invested time; not as much time would be given to relationships with other organizations. With the immigrant groups, there was informal coordination. Though they were complementary and overlapped at certain points, the core mission, policy goals, and day-to-day activities of the organizations varied.

Finally, the anti-immigrant context and past experiences with similar campaigns prompted immigrant organizations to consider different strategies for how best to be involved in the policy arena. This decision highlights how varying types of organizations involved in a coalition will engage in a different political calculus, depending on the issue. At certain times, and no matter how allied organizations are on common goals, it may be that organizations will have to act independently within a policy arena in order to preserve their core interests.

This example raises broader questions about the roles, responsibilities, and positions of organizations that have a stake in, but are not integral to, the decision-making processes of a claims-making coalition. With the defeat of Proposition 86, the CHK coalition maintained an ad hoc partnership with immigrants' rights groups. Their work together focused on the undocumented aspect of the children's coverage campaign. They continued to be allies, and have, over time, articulated specific ways of working together. For example, the California Immigrant Policy Center conducted workshops and developed resources for non-immigrant organizations to craft more effective and politically viable messages about immigrants and the undocumented. This effort to equip non-immigrant organizations with new skills and capacity specifically around this issue is an important inter-organizational development in their effort to increase the likelihood that their ultimate policy goals can be achieve. It also illustrates a structural change intended to facilitate more shared understanding and cohesion among the groups. Here again, the California Endowment responded to concerns from the organizations and supported a specific mechanism by which the organizations might be able to better collaborate.

Through the cycles of policy change and budget negotiations, the issue of health coverage for the undocumented presents two challenges for the future of statewide coalition organizing. First, cultivating organizational cohesion across groups was necessary because the types of coalitions studied were comprised of a wide range of diverse organizations with varying policy goals, strategies, and interests. Integrating the interests, goals, and strategies of groups that want to work together, yet struggle with how best to do so, is an on-going challenge among mainstream and immigrant organizations who partner in coalitions. Undocumented coverage also presents a challenge in the claims-making environment. External interest groups—whether they are heterogeneous grassroots alliances or solely immigrant rights coalitions—need to garner enough support among legislators and build momentum among voters. Likewise, these must generate enough public support to continuing pressuring public officials on the wisdom of covering all people, regardless of status.

TABLE 5: Overview of Findings	
What factors facilitated robust <u>Inter-organizational partnerships</u>?	
1. Existing relationships	▪ Foundation of organizational alliances that catalyzed initial inter-group credibility and trust/distrust.
2. Conveners	▪ Organized coalition partners, targeting diverse organizational mix with various resources and expertise. Made initial choices about political viability.
3. External funding investment	▪ Provided financial resources to support convening of coalition, coordinating staff, and campaign operations.
4. Steering committees with early agreements	▪ Decision-making structure that articulated members' roles and responsibilities, determined guiding principles for campaign goals, and developed strategy and action.
5. Internal commitments	▪ Especially for steering committee members, partners dedicated financial resources, staff, and/or "people power" for campaigns' mobilization activities.
6. Reputation and public standing	▪ Affected coalition's ability to leverage organizational allies and legislative relationships, external funding, and public support.
7. Heterogeneity	▪ Organizational diversity contributed to coalition interdependence because of varying resources and expertise. Also posed threat to cohesion with potential for internal division over incongruent interests/goals.
8. Shared mission	▪ Common agreement that access and affordability were central to coalitions' purpose. Stronger coalitions existed with greater alignment between coalition priorities and partners' goals.

TABLE 5 Cont.: Overview of Findings	
What factors contributed to Intra-organizational development?	
1. New skills and resources	▪ Individual organizations increased capacity for state policy work by acquiring new skills and resources for action.
2. Constituent mobilization among member organizations	▪ Signature gathering and legislative advocacy connected statewide policy issues to constituent participation and was opportunity to build or expand organizations' base.
3. New strategies for political action	▪ Coalition organizing led certain organizations to employ new strategies for political action that benefit future campaigns.
What factors indicate successful Claims-making by coalitions?	
1. Policy change	▪ Changes in health policy as they affect immigrants.
2. Legislative influence	▪ Demand making activity at legislature through advocacy visits, attendance at hearings, and turnout for public rallies.
3. Involvement in policy formulation & implementation	▪ Coalition partners that had voice in policy formulation and implementation strategies.

CHAPTER SEVEN

Immigrant Organizations and Policy Change: The Future Role of Coalitions

OVERVIEW

The examples of coalition activity in Massachusetts and California between 2004 and 2007 substantiate the role of grassroots alliances in policymaking. Coalitions can facilitate access to the policymaking process from an intermediary position, and thereby impact the inclusion of group political interests. In the cases studied, organizations embedded within immigrant communities engaged in coalition organizing on behalf of a constituency. Immigrants also participated in collective action through these campaigns. Even with variable gains, the coalitions exercised public influence through their demand making strategies and advanced the political capacities of coalition partners. Especially for traditionally marginalized groups, coalitions can be an effective mechanism by which immigrant-based organizations have voice and influence in the democratic process, even when building alliances across race and ethnicity, socioeconomic status, and policy issue. This chapter explores the implications of these findings for theory and practice.

A central feature of this study has been its focus on immigrant organizations that are members of statewide policy change coalitions. The examples investigate the role of these organizations outside the usual forums for immigrant organizing. This focus serves a specific purpose for theory and practice. First, the organizational conditions found in the coalition building process are presented as a conceptual framework for use in future empirical inquiry. The composite picture of inter-organizational and intra-organizational factors, and the outcomes they influenced, provides an analytic pathway for explaining how immigrant political interests can be incorporated in the policymaking process through statewide coalitions of mixed organizational type. This framework offers an organizational perspective on how and to what extent the coalitions were able to facilitate the incorporation of immigrant health interests in the policymaking process. The three sets of common factors also shed light on the ways in which the campaigns' results may have differed because of elements unique to each situation.

It is evident that the coalitions worked effectively in some ways—and not in others—to integrate immigrant interests into demand making strategies in the policy arena. This understanding illuminates how and why political coalitions can function as vehicles of democratic inclusion for newcomers (Andersen and Cohen 2005). It also contributes broader understanding of how participation in coalitions can impact the integration of immigrant interests within American political and civic life. Therefore, these conceptual ideas are also applicable to practitioners and to the implementation of organizing campaigns for social policy change.

The examples from Massachusetts and California have implications for organizations in other states that want to change public policy and for staff and organizers who work through coalitions. Where the analytic framework articulates factors that facilitate or inhibit the relationship between organizational processes and political outcomes, the findings also point to practical suggestions for how grassroots coalitions can achieve successful policy change. Specifically, recommendations made in this chapter can inform coalition-building strategies for health care organizing as well as for other immigrant-related issues, such as education policy.

IMPLICATIONS OF FINDINGS

New inter-organizational partnerships resulted from the coalition building processes observed in Massachusetts and California. Prior relationships among coalition members, the leadership of conveners, and external funding investments laid necessary groundwork for the organizational alliances to influence public policy outcomes. Early agreements made by steering committee members about roles, responsibilities, and shared principles were the foundation from which the coalitions built their campaigns and took action. This foundation was strengthened by the substantial commitment of internal resources made by partner groups that acted as anchor organizations for the larger coalitions. At critical junctures in the campaigns, the reputation and public standing of certain coalition members made it possible to leverage influential legislative relationships along with support from allies and the general public.

A diverse organizational mix and a shared mission presented opportunities for and potential threats to coalition unity and cohesion. For the immigrant advocacy organizations—those that solely identify with an immigrant constituency and those that include immigrants as one group in their membership base—these inter-organizational factors allowed them to broaden their claims and integrate the collective interests of multiple constituencies. Organizational diversity within a coalition also tested members' ability to remain committed to its core principles and to each other. With organizational diversity came the possibility that disagreements among partner groups about priorities and strategic focus could lead to fragmentation.

Leading coalition members experienced intra-organizational development as a result of the campaigns. Organizations gained new skills and resources that were acquired as a result of their participation in the campaigns. The campaigns also challenged organizations to work differently and to try out new strategies for action within the policy arena. Signature gathering and legislative advocacy events mobilized grassroots constituencies, and connected their participation in the campaigns to larger policy issues beyond local concerns. These factors contributed to growing political capacity among individual organizations. It was also particularly constructive for those community-based organizations that had not been involved previously with statewide legislative campaigns.

The implications of capacity building among immigrant-based organizations in the campaigns studied are debatable, and lend themselves to further investigation. For some of the organizations, especially those with immigrants as a part of their constituent group, the campaigns proved advantageous for base-building and internal mobilization. For others, questions remain about the extent to which health care organizing advanced their ability to be effective on future statewide campaigns. This was due in part to the fact that the health care organizing campaigns between 2004 and 2007 coincided with the 2006 mass mobilization of immigrants and immigrant organizations in the wake of HR 4437. In the future, immigrant groups will continue to balance the need to respond to proposed policies that target immigrants, and their commitment to advocating for social policies that advance immigrant health and wellbeing. Given this dynamic, it is not yet certain how well the organizational outcomes will benefit future policy campaigns for this group of organizations. Furthermore, it also remains to be seen whether or not the outcomes of the campaigns will have broader impact on the advancement and integration of immigrant rights at the local, state, and national levels.

While differential claims-making success resulted from the coalitions' public actions, they were involved directly in the policy change process through multiple activities: testimony at legislative hearings, advocacy visits to individual legislators, public rallies and press conferences, and the ballot campaigns that included signature gathering and phone banking. In both states, there were also instances of organizational involvement in policy formulation and implementation. The grassroots mobilization that linked legislative advocacy with ballot initiatives was a central demand making strategy that had capacity building implications for the coalition itself and its member organizations. This was a key indicator of successful claims-making, given this study's focus on organizational process. In addition, the direct relationships that coalition leaders developed with legislative and executive leadership are important results that will have lasting impact on future statewide policy change efforts.

Despite commonalities in the coalitions' organizational processes, the successes in California were not entirely congruent with the success found in Massachusetts. Where the coalition in Massachusetts achieved clear policy gains that would directly benefit immigrant health access, the coalitions in California had only moderate influence between 2004 and 2007. Despite repeated efforts by the Californians for Healthy Kids (CHK) Coalition, the Having Our Say (HOS) Coalition, and the It's Our Health Care (IOHC) Coalition, coverage for undocumented children had not passed as of December 2007. Three factors may account for the differences in this outcome. Here too, further investigation is needed to assess the extent to which the presence of the coalitions impacted long-term policy change outcomes, especially since the Federal reauthorization of the Children's Health Insurance Program (CHIPRA) in 2009.[48]

Most important among these factors was the difference in type of immigrant health coverage pursued, and how winnable the policy goals could be given each state's political context. Even though California has had historically   progressive   social   policies   towards

---

[48] This legislation included a provision that eliminated the five-year ban on access to coverage for legally residing immigrant children and pregnant women (Kaiser 2009). Many organizations involved in the campaigns studied between 2004 and 2007 also lobbied in support of reauthorization and the elimination of the five-year ban.

immigrants, health coverage for the undocumented is an intensely controversial public issue. The CHK Coalition made considerable gains from 2004-2007, yet they were unable to win coverage expansion for all children. At the same time, CHK's capacity for statewide organizing grew and their allied relationships with immigrant organizations strengthened. The emergence of the HOS Coalition during the statewide health reform battle created another avenue by which more immigrant-based organizations could have a unified voice around access and affordability for communities of color. Since 2007, members of the CHK and HOS coalitions have remained active in statewide and national health care campaigns, deepening their organizational connections and growing their ability to strategically influence even the most contentious policy issues. For example, members of both coalitions pursued political involvement strategies in the campaigns for CHIPRA and the proposed *Immigrant Children's Health Insurance Act* (which served as the basis for new immigrant provisions passed in CHIPRA), as well as the 2009-2010 campaigns for national health reform. These organizational developments are positive signs for the policy challenges ahead and for the continued inclusion of immigrant health interests in that process.

Second, there was fragmentation within California's advocacy community about how to mobilize support for coverage for the undocumented. Because the state's network of community-based and advocacy organizations is larger than in Massachusetts, it is not surprising that policy priorities and strategic goals varied among the different groups, especially once Governor Schwarzenegger announced his health reform plan in January 2007. Within the CHK and HOS Coalitions, there was evidence of strong, cohesive partnerships united around a shared goal. However, the presence of multiple coalitions advocating for a similar policy agenda— including that of the larger IOHC Coalition—may have contributed to the lack of claims-making success during the 2007 health reform campaigns. Third, no matter how effective and unified a coalition is, organizing campaigns are also subject to the whims of legislative action and the choices public officials make. This too may have contributed to the failed attempts at policy change in California.

The implications of these claims-making outcomes for immigrant-based organizations are extensive. Coverage proposals for immigrants in both states were linked to broader health goals: advancing a policy agenda of accessible, affordable, and quality care for immigrants was one component of an overall organizing strategy. In Massachusetts, the Massachusetts Immigrant and Refugee Advocacy Coalition, SEIU 615, SEIU 1199, and the grassroots groups, Neighbor to Neighbor MA and the Greater Boston Interfaith Organization, all had a direct stake in coverage for permanent legal residents. Collectively, they could advocate for this policy goal. That said, one respondent reflected on whether or not the varied interests of immigrants were truly represented at such a diverse coalition table. Because not everyone was an immigrant advocate, there was the potential risk of fragmentation over this issue within the ACT Coalition.

In California, a similar mix of organizations also had a direct stake in coverage for undocumented children,[49] yet

---

[49] Though it was not the focus of this case study, coverage for undocumented adults was included under the proposed health

some immigrant–based organizations were not initially included in the coalition for children's health coverage. As a result, fragmentation among these groups may have contributed to a weakened impact in the policymaking process. It is important to note that advocates and organizers faced a different political challenge in Massachusetts, where only a handful of organizations have turned their attention to covering the undocumented, and where anti-immigrant sentiment has been less pervasive than in border states, like California and Arizona.

IMPLICATIONS FOR PRACTICE

As seen in Massachusetts and California between 2004 and 2007, coalitions are subject to the capricious nature of the policy arena and legislative behavior, leaving them open to uncertainty in their operating environment. Even in unpredictable operating environments, policy influence can come from the bottom-up. Inter-organizational partnerships can build momentum over time, as grassroots actors organize around shared demand-making priorities and pressure policymakers with various tactics of collective action. In this regard, examples from the analysis found herein point to the kinds of mechanisms that can increase organizational adaptability and decrease threats to coalition cohesion and viability.

For instance, the agreements made early in the coalition building process facilitated greater cohesion in the long term. By formally agreeing to a set of principles

---

reform legislation of 2007. This same mix of organizations with a direct stake in the policy goals also grew during the campaigns for health reform.

that guided coalition activity and decision-making, the groups were able to navigate more effectively the tensions that inevitably arose as strategies were devised and public actions planned. Convening organizations and the support from external funding sources played similar roles in sustaining the coalitions. These types of lessons are directly applicable to immigrant-based organizations, and the grantmakers who support them. They are also germane to national coalition organizing, much of which has been elevated to prominence since 2007 and the election of Barack Obama in 2008.

The cases of Massachusetts and California have focused on the opportunities and challenges of coalitions whose central purpose is health policy change. These cases provide a sub-context to a larger political environment in which immigrant-based organizations seek to influence public dialogue, policy, and practice. The results of this study provide one perspective on the extent to which the interests of a marginalized group can be integrated into the political process, as well as what factors can lead to effective coalition organizing for policy influence. Many of the themes revealed in these narratives are echoed on the national stage amidst the most recent movements for immigration and health care reforms. Therefore, the findings point to a set of conditions that can also be applied at the national level. Table 6 details recommendations based on the findings from this study.

The political and organizational contexts in Massachusetts and California shaped the environment in which the coalitions organized for public action. During the time period studied, the executive and legislative leadership in both states promoted comprehensive health reform. Massachusetts and California also had well-developed networks of advocates and grassroots organizing groups that were mobilized in response to the political opportunity to influence health reform. Prior campaigns for policy change set the foundation on which these campaigns took place. For groups interested in convening coalitions, identifying similar types of pre-conditions can help to determine whether or not the time is right to embark on a statewide campaign for policy change (Roberts-DeGennaro and Mizrahi 2005).

First, a well-developed set of organizational relationships should exist that can be drawn upon for participation. Among potential members, there should be anchor organizations that are equipped with the capacity to convene a heterogeneous group of partners around common goals and a shared mission. These organizations should consider the extent to which their leadership can navigate political dynamics within the coalition leadership and with external relationships among policymakers. There should also be a mix of resources, as well as strong political standing and positive organizational reputation, among members of a proposed alliance.

Organizations that have a direct stake in the policy issue of concern and ties to related constituencies can be integral partners in campaign planning, decision making, and mobilizing for public actions. From the beginning, these organizations should be included in the planning and implementation of the alliance. There should be a firm commitment to shared purpose among partners, with a willingness to be adaptable in negotiating strategy and action. A well-defined and mutually agreed upon process for decision making that is established from the start can help to buffer potential conflict over goals, strategy, and action.

Funding for the coalition and its planned campaigns also should be negotiated early on in the process of building a new alliance. To support the coalition's work, decisions should be made about whether or not funding will come from an external source or be earmarked by members of the alliance. If funding comes solely from within the coalition, partners should discuss how this may or may not affect the overall cohesion and viability of the alliance in the long run. Finally, groups should map whether or not there is adequate political will among public officials to garner enough support for campaign goals and policy priorities. Ensuring that the coalition has strategic allies who can shore up additional resources and support is a critical step for sustainability.

There are also applicable lessons specific to immigrant-based organizations new to state level political action. First, organizations with direct ties to immigrant communities — no matter the size or scale — can have a role to play in statewide policy change efforts. Coalitions can serve as a link for this type of organization. In Massachusetts and California, organizations with a predominantly local or regional scope were able to connect their work to larger efforts through the coalitions. They built alliances with other organizations that may have looked entirely different from their own, but had a shared stake in health care access, affordability, and quality. In spite of the varying policy outcomes, these partnerships, and the opportunities that came from statewide action, built up the internal resources of smaller organizations, introducing them to new organizing strategies for political action.

The internal benefits for groups new to inter-organizational partnerships for policy change were a significant factor in their increased political capacity. Organizations new to statewide organizing can consider the following questions prior to joining a campaign:

1. In what ways will a statewide campaign help to build the internal capacity of our organization?
2. Are the campaign goals aligned with our organizational priorities?
3. How can a statewide campaign foster base building among our constituency?
4. How will a successful policy outcome benefit our constituency?
5. Do we have the necessary resources to commit to a statewide campaign?
6. What are the tradeoffs for our organization?

Finally, five organizational factors can positively impact coalition effectiveness, and should be accounted for prior to embarking on a statewide campaign. First, partnerships can accumulate greater power to impact statewide issues by relying on existing networks *and* expanding to alliances with unlikely allies. Second, conveners and steering committees are critical to maintaining cohesion. Such leadership positions should have clearly articulated roles and responsibilities. Agreements on policy priorities and goals, organizing strategies, and how the partners will work together also should be developed early in the coalition building process and evaluated along the way. All partner groups should explicitly identify what organizational commitments they can make to the campaign and to the alliance. These include financial contributions to the campaign, dedicated staff time, and the commitment of members to action. Fifth, on-going opportunities need to exist in order to sustain the direct participation of individuals affected by the issue at stake. Together, attending to these organizational factors can help to balance the impact of potential threats to cohesion that can result from emerging dynamics within the coalition or externally from within the legislative arena.

MOVING AHEAD

In the last fifteen years, statewide, pro-immigrant organizations such as the Massachusetts Immigrant and Refugee Advocacy Coalition, the California Immigrant Policy Center, the Coalition for Humane Immigrant Rights of Los Angeles, the Illinois Coalition for Immigrant and Refugee Rights, the Florida Immigrant Coalition, and the New York Immigrant Coalition have established themselves as credible advocates on social policy issues affecting immigrants and their families. Foundations and national organizations that support immigrant integration and civic participation have made targeted investments in research, organizational development, base building among immigrant constituencies, and program coordination across areas of common interest. The Grantmakers Concerned with Immigrants and Refugees, the Four Freedoms Fund, and the Center for Community Change are three such groups. They have each prioritized support for immigrant integration, seeking to develop the resources and internal capacities of community institutions and advocacy groups for effective and sustainable program implementation, including organizing for policy change.

TABLE 6: Recommendations for Practice: Coalition Building for Immigrant Policy Interests

Pre-conditions for Statewide Campaigns

- Well-developed organizational relationships exists to drawn upon for participation
- Conveners have capacity to recruit and organize heterogeneous partners with common goals and shared mission
- A mix of resources, political standing, and positive organizational reputation exists among members of alliance
- Organizations with direct stake in policy issue of concern and ties to related constituencies are integral partners in campaign planning, decision making, and mobilization for public actions
- Partners understand extent to which their leadership can navigate political dynamics within the coalition leadership and among policy makers
- A commitment to shared purpose exists among partners through mutually agreed upon principles
- There is a well-defined and mutually agreed upon process for decision making established from the start, with a willingness to negotiate and adapt strategy and action
- Funding is available to support coalition from external source or earmarked for campaign by members of alliance
- Political will exists among policymakers so that coalition can garner support for campaign goals and policy priorities

Organizational Considerations for Statewide Campaigns

- Proposed campaign can help build organization's internal capacity for political action in specific, well-defined ways.
- Campaign goals are aligned with organizational priorities.
- Statewide campaign will foster base building and leadership development among organization's constituency through campaign's political action strategies.
- A successful policy outcome can directly benefit constituency.
- Necessary resources exist within organization to commit to statewide campaign, including adequate staffing.
- Assessment of benefits outweighs potential tradeoffs for organizational participation in campaign.

| TABLE 6 Cont.: Recommendations for Practice |
| Coalition Building for Immigrant Policy Interests |
| **Tools for Building Coalition Effectiveness** |
| • Partnerships should rely on existing networks *and* expand to alliances with "unlikely allies" as long as there is clear alignment between goals and priorities of partner groups. |
| • Conveners and steering committees should have clearly articulated roles and responsibilities in order to maintain cohesion over time. |
| • Agreements on goals, policy priorities, organizing strategies, and methods for working together should be developed early in coalition building process and evaluated along the way. |
| • Partner groups should explicitly identify what organizational commitments they can make to the campaign and the alliance, including financial resources, dedicated staff time, and commitment of members to political action. |
| • On-going opportunities should exist for participation of individuals directly affected by issue at stake. |

Founded in 1990, the Grantmakers Concerned with Immigrants and Refugees (GCIR) is a network of foundations that fund programs and initiatives for newcomer communities. GCIR members cover a range of program areas, from social service delivery to policy research and advocacy. It predominantly fund initiatives in the United States, with some focus on programs abroad. Its mission is to influence philanthropy by increasing the field's awareness of issues that affect immigrant wellbeing and integration so that foundations make strategic investments based on current trends, scholarship, and best practices. GCIR also promotes the notion that philanthropy can shape public policy and the effective and coordinated delivery of services for newcomers. It emphasizes that the contributions of immigrants and refugees are central to building strong and vibrant democratic communities (McGarvey 2004).

To deepen the field's understanding of these contributions, GCIR supports its members by providing: a biennial national convening of grantmakers; research and publications on current trends and issues; strategy sessions to develop coordinated plans of action; and technical assistance through web-based tools and in-person site visits. For example, GCIR's toolkit *Investing in Our Communities: Strategies for Immigrant Integration* (Petsod, Wang and McGarvey 2006) brings together current scholarship and best practices drawing on 1) the historical context of demographic changes in the United States, 2) a theoretical framework for immigrant integration that highlights individual and institutional pathways for change; and 3) "promising practices" to inform program development. The comprehensive nature of this resource, and its grounding in theory and research, points to an important trend in philanthropy. As seen among GCIR members, funders are prioritizing multi-sector responses based on shared learning across the field for high impact practice. More and more, the philanthropic sector sees itself as a catalytic agent for social, economic, and political change.

In that vein, the Four Freedoms Fund was established in 2003 to advance the national immigrant rights field, with support from ten foundations including Carnegie Corporation of New York, the Ford Foundation, Evelyn and Walter Haas, Jr. Fund, Open Society Institute, the Horace Hagedorn Foundation, Bill and Melinda Gates Foundation, J.M. Kaplan Fund, Northwest Area Foundation, and Western Union Foundation. The Four Freedoms Fund has distributed over $23 million since its creation, focusing on three priority areas: immigration reform, immigrant civic engagement and integration, and civil liberties and human rights. Grantees cover thirty-three states and include geographic areas with either high concentrations of immigrants or growing foreign-born populations. In order to accomplish its grant-making goals, the Fund has a two-fold strategy that aims to connect coalition alliances to local grassroots groups and to national campaigns. It invests in growing organizational infrastructure for multi-year capacity building. It also encourages peer learning among grantees and provides technical assistance for development and implementation. With this type of strategy, the Fund supports coalitions as mediating structures that advance immigrant rights.

Similar to the investments made by the Four Freedoms Fund, the Center for Community Change has also prioritized capacity building for public action and coalition organizing among grassroots community organizations. Founded in 1968, the Center for Community Change has a long history of organizing and advocacy, and aims to build power and civic capacity in low-income communities and communities of color. The Center's main organizing strategy is to connect and strengthen over 200 organizations in forty states, to cultivate leadership among staff and constituencies in these organizations, to provide technical assistance for organizational development, and to mobilize groups for civic engagement and political action. Specifically, the Center attempts to engage grassroots constituencies in national policy issues. The Center for Community Change also has grown its own capacity to leverage organizational relationships across the country for policy change. Especially in the last ten years, it has taken on national anti-poverty campaigns, including jobs and employment, health care access, and immigration reform, regularly partnering with other national non-profit organizations for large-scale policy change initiatives.

One of the Center's main policy priorities has been the passage of comprehensive immigration reform. The Fair Immigration Reform Movement (FIRM) was convened by the Center in 2000 as a national coalition for immigrant rights. It is comprised of over 300 organizations, ranging from well-established, state-level immigrant rights groups, such as the Illinois Coalition for Immigrant and Refugee Rights, to smaller, ethnic-based non-profit organizations like the National Korean American Service & Education Consortium. Many of these organizations had been dealing first hand with the fallout from 1996 welfare reform as their constituents were impacted sharply by growing restrictions on eligibility and access to public benefits. FIRM is staffed by organizers from the Center, and is governed by a twenty-eight member Immigrant Organizing Committee, with a nine member Executive Committee responsible for the coalition's strategic focus.

Since its founding, the FIRM Coalition has worked on national and state issue campaigns. At the national level these include: comprehensive immigration reform, the Dream Act (to increase college access for undocumented students), and formulating a response to the rise in detentions and deportations that are a result of recent immigration raids. State and local campaigns include policies related to in-state tuition, drivers' licenses, law enforcement, public benefits, and access to citizenship services. In order to accomplish its goals, the FIRM Coalition focuses on building up the organizational infrastructure and political capacity of partner organizations (for example: supporting staff development and leadership training for political advocacy) as well as mobilizing state and local resources for involvement in national campaigns. The FIRM Coalition is, in many respects, a key pathway for local and state groups to participate in national policy change efforts.

The network of immigrant rights organizations and movement leaders across the country have tended in the past to be loosely connected with one other. The marches of 2006 in response to HR 4437 and the most recent campaigns for comprehensive immigration reform have prompted movement leaders to prioritize tighter inter-organizational alliances across groups in order to maximize impact and grow a unified voice on immigrant rights issues. For example, members of FIRM's Executive Committee are also involved with Federal immigration policy campaigns that are formed in collaboration with other national organizations who have made immigration reform a top priority such as the National Immigration Forum and the National Council of La Raza.

With progress towards federal reforms in immigration and health care policy, the activities of the Four Freedoms Fund and the Center for Community Change have catalyzed broader alliances that respond to and advocate for policies directly impacting immigrant constituencies. They have aligned themselves with other state and national organizations in an effort to influence Federal policy debates. The successful reauthorization of children's health insurance was one occasion in which national and state organizations came together around a shared policy agenda that advanced immigrant health coverage. Several of the organizations involved in the 2004-2007 Massachusetts and California campaigns successfully mobilized advocacy efforts for the *Immigrant*

Children's Health Improvement Act, adopted as a provision within the new CHIRPA law. This included expansion of coverage for at least 400,000 immigrant children.

CONCLUSION

The current national campaigns for immigration and health care reform have increased the salience of this study's findings, their implications for practice, and the recommendations made above. This study has been an occasion to examine a contemporary policy and political action phenomenon with the goal of building a theoretical framework about coalitions as instruments of policy change. It has explored one dimension of immigrant political incorporation with the intent of contributing both analytic tools and practical knowledge to the study of community organizing, health policy change, and immigrant political activism. Given the current debates about health care access, immigration control, and comprehensive policy reform, the findings hold yet one more conclusion that crosses both theory and practice.

Immigrant-based organizations — those that organize immigrants and those that advocate on their behalf — are on the front lines of the national dialogue about the rights and privileges of newcomers in the United States. Staff and organizers of these organizations daily confront the challenges inherent in this environment, where newcomers continue to live in fear about their safety and the well-being of their families and communities. Likewise, the inclusion of immigrant political interests in today's policy arena stands on tentative ground. Both realities present opportunities for future investigation, seeking new ways of understanding how immigrant organizations navigate the challenges of this terrain.

Even amidst the anti-immigrant trends in the United States today, the organizations interviewed for this study, and the coalitions they formed for policy change, are a hopeful sign.   As a necessary vehicle for 21st century politics,   these   claims-making   coalitions   and   their organizational partners willingly put themselves on the line so that their immigrant members have access to the resources and supports they need for healthy and stable lives   in   their   new   homeland.   Looking   ahead,   the continued growth of these alliances, their development of political capacity, and their ability to leverage public influence across varying communities of interest holds great   promise   for   the   meaningful   participation   and inclusion of immigrants in American democracy.

Appendix 1: Sample Interview Protocols

Massachusetts
1. Why did you choose to mobilize others around immigrant health coverage and access to Medicaid benefits?
    a. What opportunity or threat did State action imply?
    b. Was the issue's resolution the primary end or primarily an occasion to mobilize?
    c. What other issues have you tried to mobilize (immigrant) communities around?

2. How did you decide to get involved in this policy issue?
    a. Did you have a specific decision making process? When was the decision made?
    b. What sources of information did you use to decide? (Media, scanning of legislation, personal contacts)
    c. How did you figure out how immigrants feel about the issue?
    (Information sources and modes of communication)

3. Which immigrant communities were most involved?
    a. When did they get involved?
    b. Had they been involved before? If so, in what?
4. What were the backgrounds and experience of immigrant leaders involved?
5. How have you chosen partners for the campaign?
    a. Had you worked with them before? On what?
    b. What characteristics did you seek among partner organizations?
    c. Were organizations added later in the process? Why?
    d. Were there organizations that should have been involved that were not? Why?

6. What kinds of strategies did you use in the campaign?
    a. To influence the policy process
    b. To mobilize partner organizations and immigrants

7. How did you decide on those strategies?
   a. What alternative issues did you consider? Why did you reject them?
8. Who participated in setting the agenda and developing the campaign strategy?
   a. What are the roles and responsibilities of immigrants, paid staff, non-immigrant volunteers?
   b. How did you maintain communications with organizational partners?

Impact
Legislative:
9. Who were the key decision-makers involved?
   a. Had you had prior occasion to interact with them?
10. How has this campaign impacted your relationship with legislators and other decision makers?
11. What was the decision making process at the legislature and how did you deal with it? (ex: committees, leadership decisions)
    a. What seems to be the key factors in the decision?
    b. Difference between informal and formal legislative decisions?
    c. If informal: Did you have any influence on these decisions?
12. How did timing of legislative process affect planning the mobilization effort?

Organizational:
13. Did you change anything within <<your organization>> for the campaign or as a result of what has happened since the campaign started?
    a. Are there new structures/processes in place as a result of this campaign?
    b. How have new structures/processes benefited the organization?
    c. In what ways will structures/processes benefit your future work?

Partners/Constituency:

14. What impact has organizing effort had on your relationship with your constituency?
15. Has the campaign fostered better relationships with other organizations and partners? How?

16. What have you learned from this campaign?
    a. How have these lessons informed future organizing strategies?
    b. Did lessons from past campaigns inform your strategy with the <XX> campaign?
17. Who else do you recommend I talk with?
18. Do you have any questions for me?

California
Questions in bold were added after January 2007 announcement

1. Tell me about your organization. What do you do? Who are your members? How do you organize?
2. Describe your role in current campaign?
    a. Is it new work for your organization? Similar to efforts in the past?
    b. What are goals?
3. How did coalition come together?
    a. Who else are you working with?
    b. What agreements have you made? How did you make them?
    c. Have you worked with partners in the past?
    d. Process for picking partners? Who convened?
    e. **What about the other coalitions? Do you work together? Do you have a sense of their goals?**

4. Why this issue? How did your organization decide to get involved?

5.   What kinds of strategies for this campaign?
     a.   How did you make decisions?
     b.   Who is involved?
     c.   Who is involved in policy formulation? Is it possible for outside groups to influence? How?
     d.   **Has the Governor's announcement altered your state-wide strategy?**

6.   Has anything change within your organization for this campaign?
     a.   Are there new structures/processes in place as a result of this campaign?
     b.   How have they benefited the organization/future campaigns?

7.   What impact has organizing effort had on your relationship with your membership/constituent organizations?

8.   Has your relationship with other organizations and partners changed because of this work? How?

9.   Impact on relationships with legislators and key decision makers?

10. What have you learned from this campaign?

11. Who else do you recommend I talk with?

12. Do you have any questions for me?

Appendix 2: Coalition Member Lists

MIRACLE Coalition Organizational Members (since 2004)
Public Policy Institute (Convener)
Health Care for All
Latin American Health Institute
Massachusetts Immigrant and Refugee Advocacy Coalition
The Massachusetts Law Reform Institute
SEIU 615/Voice and Future Fund (501c3)

Miracle Campaign Endorsers
Beth Israel Deaconess Medical Center
Boston Medical Center
Boston Public Health Commission
Centro Presente
Codman Square Health Center
Community Partners
Dorchester House Multi-Service Center
Greater Boston Chinese Golden Age Center
Greater New Bedford Community Health Center
Jewish Community Relations Council
Latino Health Institute
Lowell Community Health Center
Lynn Community Health Center
Massachusetts Association of Jewish Federations
Massachusetts Hospital Association
Massachusetts Jobs with Justice
Muslim American Society Freedom Foundation
Neighbor to Neighbor MA
Sisters Together Ending Poverty
Uphams Corner Health Center

ACT Coalition Organizational Members (as of 12/2006)
Health Care for All (Convener)
American Cancer Society
American Heart / American Stroke Association
Artists Foundation, Inc.
Boston Center for Independent Living

ACT Coalition Organizational Members (as of 12/2006) cont.
Boston Medical Center
Boston Public Health Commission
Cambridge Health Alliance
Children's Hospital Boston
Children's Health Access Coalition
Coalition for Social Justice
Families USA
Greater Boston Interfaith Organization
Health Law Advocates
Home Care Alliance of Massachusetts
Massachusetts Academy of Family Physicians
Massachusetts Building Trades Council
Massachusetts Business Leaders for Quality, Affordable Health Care
Massachusetts Chapter of the American Academy of Pediatrics
Massachusetts College of Emergency Physicians
Massachusetts Community Action Network
Massachusetts Community Health Worker Network
Massachusetts Council of Community Hospitals
Massachusetts Immigrant and Refugee Advocacy Coalition
Massachusetts Health Council
Massachusetts Hospital Association
Massachusetts Law Reform Institute
Massachusetts League of Community Health Centers
Massachusetts Medical Society
Massachusetts NOW
Massachusetts Public Health Association
Mental Health and Substance Abuse Corporations of MA
Neighbor to Neighbor MA
Partners HealthCare
Public Policy Institute
SEIU 615
SEIU 1199
Tobacco Free Mass
UMass Memorial Health Care
Western Mass Health Access Coalition

Californians for Healthy Kids Coalition (since 2002)
PICO CA
100% Campaign:
Children Now
The Children's Partnership
The Children's Defense Fund

Yes on Proposition 86 **Campaign Sponsors and Supporters**
(as of 9/2006)

Sponsors
American Cancer Society
American Lung Association of California
American Heart Association
California Hospital Association
The Children's Partnership
Children Now
Tobacco-Free Kids Action Fund
California Emergency Nurses Association
Association of California Nurse Leaders
PICO California
California Primary Care Association
American College of Emergency Physicians, California Chapter
Emergency and Acute Care Medical Corporation

Yes on Proposition 86 Supporters included over 300 elected officials, local government entities, professional groups, community, non-profit, and health care organizations, associations, clinics and hospitals. The following members of other coalitions were also supporters of the Yes on Proposition 86 Campaign:
Asian and Pacific Islander American Health Forum
California Black Health Network
California Pan-Ethnic Health Network
Latino Coalition for a Healthy California
Health Access
Children's Defense Fund—California (*signed on as supporter, but not as sponsor)

Having Our Say Coalition (as of 9/2007)
California Immigrant Policy Center (Convener)
California Pan-Ethnic Health Network (Convener)
Latino Issues Forum (Convener)

ACLU of Southern California
American Cancer Society, California Division, Inc
Applied Research Center
Asian and Pacific Islander American Health Forum
Asian Health Services
Asian Pacific Community Health Organization
Bay Area Immigrant Rights Coalition
California Black Health Network
California Catholic Conference
California Latinas for Reproductive Justice
California Optometric Association
California Partnership
California Rural Indian Health board
California Rural Legal Assistance Foundation
Central Valley Partnership
Centro Binacional Para el Desarrollo Indigena Oaxaqueno, Inc
Chinatown Service Center
Coalition for Humane Immigrant Rights of Los Angeles
Filipino American Service Group, Inc
The Greenlining Institute
K.W. Lee Center for Leadership
Korean Resource Center
Latino Coalition for a Health California
Latino Health Alliance
Madera Coalition for Community Justice
National Health Law Program
National Immigrant Law Center
New Alliance Organizing Project
Out of Many, One
PALS for Health
Pat Brown Institute, Health Policy Outreach Center

Services, Immigrant Rights, and Education Network
South Asian Network
The Opportunity Agenda
Vision y Compomiso/Promotora Network

It's Our Health Care Coalition (as of 2/2008)
* denotes overlap with HOS Coalition
Access | Women's Health Rights Coalition
AIDS Foundation, Orange County
Alameda Health Consortium
Amalgamated Transit Union Local 1704
AARP -- California
American Civil Liberties Union of Southern California
American Federation of State, County and Municipal Employees
American Federation of Teachers Local 2121
American Federation of Television & Radio Artists
Arts Forum San Francisco
*Asian & Pacific Islander American Health Forum
*Asian Health Services
Asian Immigrant Women Advocates
Black Women Organized for Political Action
Black Political Council of the Central Valley
California ACORN
California Alliance for Retired Americans
California Arts Advocates
California Association of Non-Profits
*California Black Health Network, Inc.
California Black Women's Health Project
California Council of Churches IMPACT
*California Immigrant Policy Center
California Labor Federation
California National Organization for Women
*California Pan-Ethnic Health Network
*California Partnership
CalPIRG
California Primary Care Association
California State Employees Association

It's Our Health Care Coalition (as of 2/2008) cont.

California Teachers Association
Capitol Area Progressives
Catholic Charities -- Diocese of Fresno
Center for Community Advocacy
Center for Third-World Organizing
Center on Policy Initiatives
Center on Race, Poverty and the Environment
Central California Forum on Refugee Affaris
Central Coast Alliance United for a Sustainable Economy
Central Coast Center for Independent Living
Chinatown Medical Clinic and Midwifery, Fresno
Clergy & Laity United for Economic Justice of California
Communications Workers of America Local 9408
Community Clinic Consortium
Community Health Councils, Inc.
Concerns Committee of Mennonite Community, Fresno
Congress of California Seniors
Consumer Federation of California
Consumers Union
Council on American Islamic Relations
Dolores Huerta Foundation
Fairview Community Church
Filipinos for Affirmative Action
Fresno Center for New Americans
Greater Richmond Interfaith Program
*Greenlining Institute
Health Access California
Hunger Action Los Angeles
Independent Living Resource Center, San Francisco
Inland Empire Working Families Coalition
Kern Minority Contractors Association
*Korean Resource Center
Koreatown Immigrant Workers Alliance
*Latino Coalition for a Healthy California
Latino Diabetes Association
*Latino Issues Forum

It's Our Health Care Coalition (as of 2/2008) cont.
Libreria del Pueblo, Inc.
LifeLong Medical Care
Los Amigos of Orange County
Los Angeles County Federation of Labor, AFL-CIO
Lutheran Office of Public Policy -- California
NAACP, Fresno
National Council of La Raza
Orange County Employees Association
Office and Professional Employees International Union Local 3
Older Women's League of California
Planned Parenthood Affiliates of California
Poverty Matters
Progressive Jewish Alliance
Progressive Christians Uniting
Sacramento Community Clinic Consortium
Saint Anselm's Episcopal Church, Garden Grove
San Bernardino Public Employees Association
Senior Action Network
Service Employees International Union
Social Justice Committee of Mennonite Community
Southeast Asia Resource Action Center
Southern California Chapter of Americans for Democratic Action
State Center Federation of Teachers, Fresno
Theatre Bay Area
United Educators of San Francisco CFT/CTA #61, AFL-CIO
United Methodist Church, Whittier
Unitarian Universalist Legislative Ministry of California
Unitarian Universalist Social Justice Committee of Fresno
Unite HERE Local 2
United Food and Commercial Workers Local 8 Golden State
United Food and Commercial Workers Local 648
Valley Medical Group
The Wall Las Memorias Project

Appendix 3: Profiles of Featured Organizations

Massachusetts

Coalition for Social Justice
The Coalition for Social Justice is a multi-issue organization that advocates for public policies to improve the lives of ordinary people. Based in Southeastern Massachusetts, CSJ combines policy advocacy with grassroots campaigns for economic and social justice issues.

Greater Boston Interfaith Organization
The Greater Boston Interfaith Organization is a multi-issue, broad-based community organization comprised of seventy member institutions (with approximately 50,000 individuals) including religious congregations, community development corporations, unions and other civic organizations. GBIO is an affiliate of the national community organizing network, the Industrial Areas Foundation.

Health Care for All
Health Care for All is the leading health-consumer, policy advocacy and education organization in Massachusetts. In addition to its policy advocacy for and monitoring of accessible and affordable health care policy options, HCFA's programs aim to reduce the rates of uninsured by increasing access and enrollment through outreach and education. Health Care for All convened the ACT Coalition and was a member of the MIRACLE Campaign.

Neighbor to Neighbor MA
Neighbor to Neighbor MA organizes low-income and working people to have a voice on issues of economic justice. Their program areas include voter registration and education, candidate endorsements, public policy advocacy, coalition building, and the development of sustainable grassroots leadership.

Massachusetts Immigrant and Refugee Advocacy Coalition
The Massachusetts Immigrant and Refugee Advocacy Coalition is made up over one hundred immigrant and refugee community organizations across Massachusetts. Policy advocacy, organizing and leadership development, and education are core elements of their work.

Public Policy Institute
The Public Policy Institute trains and supports to non-profit organizations working for social and economic justice. PPI provides training in policy advocacy, campaign planning, and constituent organizing to help develop skills for successful policy change. The Public Policy Institute was the convener of the MIRACLE Campaign and a member of the ACT Coalition.

SEIU Local 615/ Voice and Future Fund (501c3)
SEIU Local 615 represents building service workers in Massachusetts, New Hampshire, and Rhode Island. The Voice and Future Fund is the non-profit partner of Local 615 focused on health and education outreach, and employment training. It also provides leadership development and policy advocacy training for low-wage workers.

SEIU 1199, United Healthcare Workers East
SEIU 1199 represents health care workers in Massachusetts, New York, Washington DC, and Maryland. Primary issue areas include quality healthcare for workers and their patients, employer responsibility for healthcare, living wage laws, and immigrant rights. In Massachusetts, SEIU 1199 represents over 12,000 members.

California

The California Immigrant Policy Center
The California Immigrant Policy Center is a non-partisan, non-profit statewide organization. Through education, research, advocacy, training, and outreach, CIPC works with policy makers, community members and advocates to advance public policies that support the wellbeing of California's immigrants and families. CIPC is a project of the Asian Pacific American Legal Center, the National Immigration Law Center, the Coalition for Humane Immigrant Rights of Los Angeles, and Services, Immigrant Rights and Education Network of San Jose, and was a convening partner of the Having Our Say Coalition and a member of the It's Our Health Care Coalition.

California Pan-Ethnic Health Network
The California Pan-Ethnic Health Network is a multicultural health policy advocacy organization. It is a partnership between the Asian & Pacific Islander American Health Forum, California Black Health Network, California Rural Indian Health Board, and Latino Coalition for a Healthy California. CPEHN aims to improve health care access and eliminate health disparities for communities of color through its advocacy, research and outreach. CPEHN was a founding partner of the Having Our Say Coalition and a member of the It's Our Health Care Coalition.

The California Partnership
The California Partnership is a statewide coalition that organizes and advocates for programs and policies that aim to reduce and end poverty. It is comprised of five chapters and over 120 community-based organizations, with a coordinating committee that guides its grassroots organizing, leadership development and training, mini-grants for capacity building, and state policy advocacy work. The California Partnership is a project of the Center for Community Change, and a member of both the Having Our Say Coalition and the It's Our Health Care Coalition.

The Children's Defense Fund California
The Children's Defense Fund California is a state affiliate of the national non-profit organization. In California, CDF-CA works to improve access to comprehensive, affordable health coverage, head start and child care. Its main tools for action include legislative and administrative advocacy, public education campaigns, and partnerships with labor, business, advocacy and community-based organizations. CDFA-CA is a member of the 100% campaign and a partner in the Californians for Healthy Kids Coalition.

Children Now
Children Now is a non-partisan, public policy advocacy organization focused on children's well-being. Its priority areas include children's health access, education, children and the media, and policy research. Children Now is a member of the 100% Campaign and a partner in the Californians for Healthy Kids Coalition.

The Children's Partnership

The Children's Partnership is a national, nonprofit advocacy organization that focuses broadly on children in underserved communities, especially on health coverage for the uninsured and the availability of technology to children and their families. TCP advances its mission through its research on best practices in local communities, which then informs a policy and advocacy agenda for change. TCP is a member of the 100% Campaign a partner in the Californians for Healthy Kids Coalition.

Coalition for Humane Immigrant Rights of Los Angeles

The Coalition for Human Immigrant Rights of Los Angeles seeks to advance the human and civil rights of immigrants and refugees at the local, state and national level. CHIRLA works to empower immigrants and their allies through coalition building, policy advocacy, community education, and grassroots organizing. CHIRLA is a partner organization of the California Immigrant Policy Center, and a member of the Having Our Say Coalition and the It's Our Health Care Coalition.

Health Access

Health Access California is the leading health consumer organization in California with a broad base of 200 member organizations. Health Access works with both community-based organizations through grassroots education and outreach, and with policy makers to advocate for health care reform. The organization is a 501(c)(4) non-profit, and was the lead convening partner of the It's Our Health Care Coalition.

Korean Resource Center

The Korean Resource Center is a non-profit organization of Korean Americans with funding from public and private sources. Based in Los Angeles, the organization mixes social service programming with outreach, advocacy, and civic engagement campaigns for health access, education, cultural exchange, and immigrant rights. The Korean Resource Center is a member of both the Having Our Say Coalition and the It's Our Health Care Coalition.

Latino Coalition for a Healthy California

The Latino Coalition for a Healthy California is a statewide organization focused on Latino health. Through research, community education and public policy advocacy LCHC seeks to address access to care, health disparities, and community health. Its network is comprised of health care providers, consumers and advocates in community-base and organizations across California. Latino Coalition for a Healthy California is a member of both the Having Our Say Coalition and the It's Our Health Care Coalition.

Latino Issues Forum

The Latino Issues Forum is a non-profit public policy and advocacy organization focused on those issues affecting California's Latino population. Through research and policy advocacy, LIF works to establish public policy solutions that address the wellbeing of Latinos in California, especially in the areas of health, education, consumer protections, sustainable development and technology. Latino Issues Forum was a convening member of the Having Our Say Coalition.

PICO California

PICO CA is an alliance of nineteen congregation-based federations in California that brings its members' issues of concern to the statewide policy arena. These issue areas include healthcare access, affordable housing, education, safe streets, and voting, and are rooted in their constituents' interests and concerns. PICO CA is an affiliate of PICO National Network, a network of faith-based community organizations in seventeen states, and over 150 cities in the United States. PICO CA is a partner in the Californians for Healthy Kids Campaign.

Appendix 4: Sample Coalition Agreements

The following summaries of coalition agreements and shared principles are from publicly available campaign documents. Additional campaign materials available upon request of Author.

MIRACLE Coalition Operating Assumptions

- Collaboration across constituencies contributes to strong campaigns.
- Effective campaigns require resources, and there is a commitment to seek the necessary resources acknowledging that community-based organizations and consumer organizations have fewer financial resources than providers; fundraising strategies will not interfere with funding for core operations of collaborating partners.
- The areas in which coordination or economies of scale make sense is common research, message development, national or regional fundraising, and any other needs specifically identified by the steering committee.

**The operating assumptions were complemented by a set of "ground rules" that partner organizations agreed to follow throughout the life of the campaign.
Source:
http://www.realclout.org/ppi/activities/Miracle/Miracle-preCampaign.stm

ACT! Coalition Principles

- MassHealth restoration and expansion
- Cost relief to moderate-income, working families including sliding-scale subsidies for private insurance
- Fair payment rates for doctors, hospitals, and other providers of MassHealth services
- Meaningful employer responsibility
- Assistance to small businesses
- Control cost growth
- Fair and sustainable funding

Source: campaign documents, Wcislo et al. (2007)

Californians for Healthy Kids Coalition Goals
- Create a strong private/public initiative in which all children living in California from birth to age 21 will have access to affordable health insurance coverage.
- Build upon what works in California's publicly-funded state insurance programs and reform what does not, including modernizing and simplifying how children get enrolled and stay enrolled in coverage.
- Create a statewide insurance system that leverages the lessons and successes of local children's health initiatives.
- Promote voluntary opportunities to strengthen employer participation in covering dependents.
- Develop sustainable financing that supports the system over the long term, including maximizing federal funding.
- Promote opportunities for children to access services under their health insurance coverage.
- Ensure a strong safety net as a vital component of access to care.
- Do no harm as these reforms are put in place.

Source:http://www.100percentcampaign.org/issues/cahealthy kids/index.htm

Having Our Say Coalition Health Care Principles
- Provide universal and affordable health care coverage for all Californians
- Assure access to equitable, high quality care for all
- Ensure equity of responsibility based on financial resources
- Assure an efficient health care system to sustain universal coverage
- Prioritize the creation of health communities

Source: http://www.cpehn.org/havingoursay.php

It's Our Health Care Coalition Principles

- Quality, affordable healthcare that allows all Californians to get the healthcare they need when they need it.
- Insurance reforms to control costs and allow everyone access to quality healthcare and coverage.
- Employers and government sharing responsibility and risk with consumers.
- Limits on the risk and burdens placed on individual consumers and families, and protecting them from being forced to buy coverage they cannot afford and that does not cover their healthcare needs.
- Prevention and safety efforts to help individuals get healthy and stay healthy, by providing healthy communities and choices, while not placing financial barriers to care.
- Policies to preserve and strengthen the public hospitals, emergency rooms, and trauma centers that all Californians rely on.
- Efforts to control costs, while protecting benefits and preventing increased financial barriers to care.

Source: www.itsourhealthcare.org/about.html

References

Andersen, Kristi, and Elizabeth F. Cohen. 2005. Political institutions and incorporation of immigrants. In *The politics of democratic inclusion*, ed. Christina Wolbrecht and Rodney E. Hero, 186-205. Philadelphia: Temple University Press.

Applied Research Center. 2002. *Mapping the immigrant infrastructure*. Oakland, CA: Applied Research Center.

Bass, Loretta E., and Lynne M. Casper. 1999. Are there differences in registration and voting behavior between naturalized and native-born Americans? U.S. Census Bureau, Population Division Working Paper #28. http://www.census.gov/population/www/documentation/twps0028/twps0028.html

Baum, Joel A.C., and Andrew V. Shipilov. 2006. Ecological approaches to organizations. In *The sage handbook of organization studies*, ed. Stewart Clegg, Cynthia Hardy, Thomas Lawrence, and Walter R. Nord, 55-110. London: Sage Publications.

Belluck, Pam and Katie Zezima. 2006. "Massachusetts legislation on insurance becomes law." *The New York Times*, April 13, A13.

Berry, Jeffrey M., Kent E. Portney, and Ken Thomson. 1993. *The rebirth of urban democracy*. Washington D.C.: The Brookings Institute.

Bloemraad, Irene. 2006. *Becoming a citizen: Incorporating immigrants and refugees in the United States and Canada*. Berkeley, CA: University of California Press.

Bolman, Lee G., and Terrence E. Deal. 2008. *Reframing organizations: Artistry, choice, and leadership*. 4th ed. San Francisco: Jossey-Bass Publishers.

Bolman, Lee G., and Terrence E Deal. 1997. *Reframing organizations: Artistry, choice and leadership*. 2nd ed. San Francisco: Jossey-Bass Publishers.

Bouman, John. 2005. The power of working with community organizations: The Illinois FamilyCare campaign—effective results through collaboration. *Clearinghouse REVIEW Journal of Poverty Law and Policy.* January-February.

Bouman, John. 2006. The path to universal health coverage for children in Illinois. *Clearinghouse REVIEW Journal of Poverty Law and Policy.* March–April.

Boyte, Harry C. and Nancy N. Kari. 1996. *Building America: The democratic promise of public work.* Philadelphia: Temple University Press.

Brown, E. Richard, Nadereh Pourat, and Steven P. Wallace. 2007. Undocumented residents make up small share of California's uninsured population. Health Policy Fact Sheet. A publication of the UCLA Center for Health Policy Research. March.
http://www.healthpolicy.ucla.edu/pubs/files/UninUndoc_FS_032807.pdf

Bueker, Catherine Simpson. 2006. *From immigrant to naturalized citizen: Political incorporation in the United States.* New York: LFB Scholarly Pub. LLC.

Capps, Randolph, Michael E. Fix, Everett Henderson, and Jane Reardon-Anderson. 2005. A profile of low-income working immigrant families. *New Federalism: National Survey of America's Families.* No. B-67: (June 30) Washington D.C.: The Urban Institute. http://www.urban.org/url.cfm?ID=311206

Capps, Randolph, Rosa Maria Castaneda, Ajay Chaudry, and Robert Santos. 2007. Paying the price: the impact of immigration raids on America's children. National Council of La Raza. (October 31).
http://www.urban.org/url.cfm?ID=411566

Carnegie Corporation. 2003. *The house we all live in: A report on immigrant civic integration.* New York: Carnegie Corporation of New York.

Clawson, Dan. 2003. *The next upsurge: Labor and the new social movements.* Ithaca: Cornell University Press.

Community Catalyst. 2006. Massachusetts health reform: What it does; how it was done; challenges ahead. Briefing Paper, April. Boston, MA.

http://www.communitycatalyst.org/resource.php?base_id=102
3

Craig, Gary, Marilyn Taylor, and Tessa Parkes. 2004. Protest or partnership? The voluntary and community sectors in the policy process. *Social Policy & Administration*. 38(3) (June): 221-239.

Crenson, Matthew A., and Benjamin Ginsberg. 2002. *Downsizing democracy: How America sidelined its citizens and privatized its public*. Baltimore: The Johns Hopkins University Press.

Crowley, Eve., Stephan Baas, Paola Termine, John Rouse, Pamela Pozarny, and Geneviève Dionne. 2007. Organizations of the poor: Conditions for success. In *Membership-based organizations of the poor*, ed. Martha Chen, Renana Jhabvala, Ravi Kanbur, and Carol Richards. 23-42. New York: Routledge.

De Graauw, Els 2008. Nonprofit organizations: Agents of immigrant political incorporation in urban America. In *Civic hopes and political realities: Immigrants, community organizations, and political engagement*, ed. S. Karthick Ramakrishnan and Irene Bloemraad, 323-350. New York: Russell Sage Foundation.

DeSipio, Louis, Natalie Masuoka, and Christopher Stout. 2006. The changing non-voter: What differentiates non-voters and voters in Asian American and Latino communities? UC Irvine: Center for the Study of Democracy. http://www.escholarship.org/uc/item/3n67v86t

DeSipio, Louis. 2000. The dynamo of urban growth: Immigration, naturalization, and the restructuring of urban politics. In *Minority politics at the millennium*. Vol. 9 of *Contemporary Urban Affairs*, ed. Richard A. Keiser and Katherine Underwood, 77-108. New York: Garland Publishing.

-----. 2001. Building America, one person at a time: Naturalization and political behavior of the naturalized in contemporary American politics." In *E pluribus unum?: Contemporary and historical perspectives on immigrant political incorporation*, ed. Gary Gerstle and John Mollenkopf, 67-106. New York: Russell Sage Foundation.

-----. 2002. Immigrant organizing, civic outcomes: Civic engagement, political activity, national attachment, and identity in Latino immigrant communities. Center for the Study of Democracy. Paper 02-08. Irvine: University of California. http://repositories.cdlib.org/csd/02-08

De Souza Briggs, Xavier. 2008. Democracy as problem solving: Civic capacity in communities across the globe. Cambridge: MIT Press.

Deutsch, Ted. 2008. Investing in change: Why supporting advocacy makes sense for foundations. *Atlantic Reports.* (May) The Atlantic Philanthropies.
http://www.atlanticphilanthropies.org/sites/default/files/uploads/ATLP_advocacy_report.pdf

Diaz, William A. 1996. Latino participation in American associational and political roles. *Hispanic Journal of Behavioral Science*: 18(2): 154-174.

Dreier, Peter, John Mollenkopf, and Todd Swanstrom. 2001. *Place matters: Metropolitics for the twenty-first century.* Lawrence, KS: University Press of Kansas.

Edwards, Michael. 2004. *Civil society.* Cambridge: Polity Press.

Eisenhardt, Kathleen M. 1989. Building theories from case study research. *The Academy of Management Review.* 14(4): 532-550.

-----, and Melissa E. Graebner. 2007. Theory building from cases: Opportunities and challenges. *The Academy of Management Journal* 50(1): 25 – 32.

Ellwood, Marilyn R. and Leighton Ku. 1998. "Welfare and immigration reforms: Unintended side effects for Medicaid." *Health Affairs.* 17(3) (May/June): 137-151.

Fix, Michael E., Jeffrey S. Passel, and Kenneth Sucher. 2003. Trends in naturalization. *Immigrant Families and Workers: Facts and Perspectives.* Research Brief, No. 3, Washington D.C.: Urban Institute.
http://www.urban.org/url.cfm?ID=310847

Fix, Michael. 2002. Do we need an integration policy? Guberman Lecture, Brandeis University. October 23.

Flores, William. 1997. Mujeres en huelga: Cultural citizenship and gender empowerment in a cannery strike. In *Latino cultural citizenship: Claiming identity, space and rights*, ed. William Flores and Rina Benmayor, 210-254. Boston: Beacon Press.

Foster-Fishman, Pennie G., Shelby L. Berkowitz, David W. Lounsbury, Stephanie Jacobson, and Nicole A. Allen. 2001. Building collaborative capacity in community coalitions: A review and integrative framework. *American Journal of Community Psychology*. 29(2) (April): 241-261.

Fremstad, Shawn, and Laura Cox. 2004. Covering new Americans: A review of federal and state policies related to immigrants' eligibility and access to publicly funded health insurance. November. Washington, D.C.: Kaiser Commission on Medicaid and the Uninsured. http://www.kff.org/medicaid/upload/Covering-New-Americans-A-Review-of-Federal-and-State-Policies-Related-to-Immigrants-Eligibility-and-Access-to-Publicly-Funded-Health-Insurance-Report.pdf

Fronstin, Paul. 2007. *Snapshot: California's Uninsured*. Oakland: California HealthCare Foundation. http://www.chcf.org/documents/insurance/SnapshotUninsured07.pdf

Ganz, Marshall. 2008. Tools for organizing: leadership, community and power. Kennedy School of Government, Harvard University. http://ksghome.harvard.edu/~mganz/PAL%20110_ORGNOTES_f2008.doc

-----. 2000. Resources and resourcefulness: Strategic capacity in the unionization of California agriculture, 1959-1966. *The American Journal of Sociology*. 105(4) (January): 1003-1062.

García Coll, Cynthia, Gontran Lamberty, Renee Jenkins, Harriet Pipes McAdoo, Keith Crnic, Barbara Hanna Wasik, and Heidie Vázquez García. 1996. An integrative model for the study of developmental competencies in minority children. *Child Development*. 67(5) (October): 1891-1914.

Gecan, Michael. 2002. *Going public*. Boston: Beacon Press.

George, Alexander L., and Andrew Bennett. 2005. *Case studies and theory development in the social sciences.* Cambridge: MIT Press.

Gerstle, Gary and John Mollenkopf. 2001. The political incorporation of immigrants, then and now. In *e pluribus unum?: Contemporary and historical perspectives on immigrant political incorporation,* ed. Gary Gerstle and John Mollenkopf, 1-30. New York: Russell Sage Foundation.

Gilbertson, Greta and Audrey Singer. 2003. The emergence of protective citizenship in the USA: Naturalization among Dominican immigrants in the post-1996 welfare reform era. *Ethnic and Racial Studies.* 26(1): 25-51.

Goodnough, Abby. 2009a. Massachusetts takes a step back from health care for all. *The New York Times.* July 15.

-----. 2009b. Massachusetts cuts back immigrants' health care. *The New York Times.* September 1.

Granovetter, Mark S. 1973. The strength of weak ties. *The American Journal of Sociology.* May. 78(6): 1360-1380.

Greater Boston Interfaith Organization. 2007. *Mandating health care insurance: What is truly affordable for Massachusetts families?* Unpublished report.

HR 4437. [109th]. Border Protection, Antiterrorism, and Illegal Immigration Control Act of 2005 (Referred to Senate Committee after being Received from House). http://frwebgate.access.gpo.gov/cgi-bin/getdoc.cgi?dbname=109_cong_bills&docid=f:h4437rfs.txt.pdf

Hardy-Fanta, Carol. 1993. *Latina politics, latino politics: Gender, culture, and political participation in Boston.* Philadelphia: Temple University Press.

Hirota, Sherry, Jane Garcia, Ralph Silber, Ingrid Lamirault, Luella J. Penserga, and Margo B. Hall. 2006. Inclusion of immigrant families in U.S. health coverage expansions. *Journal of Health Care for the Poor and Underserved.* 17(1) (February Supplement): 81-94.

Hoefer, Michael, Rytina, Nancy, and Baker, Brian C. 2009. Estimates of the unauthorized immigrant population

residing in the United States: January 2008. Office of Immigration Statistics, Department of Homeland Security. (February):
http://www.dhs.gov/xlibrary/assets/statistics/publications/ois_ill_pe_2008.pdf.

Hoffman, Beatrix. 2003. "Health care reform and social movements in the United States." *American Journal of Public Health*. 93(1) (January): 75-85.

Hojnacki, Marie. 1998. "Organized interests' advocacy behavior in alliances." *Political research quarterly*, 51(2): 437-459.

Huberman, A. Michael and Matthew B. Miles. 1994. Data management and analysis methods. In *Handbook of Qualitative Research*, ed. Norman K. Denzin and Yvonna S. Lincoln: 428-444. Thousand Oaks: Sage Publications.

Jackson-Elmoore, Cynthia. 2005. Informing state policymakers: Opportunities for social workers. *Social Work*, 50(3) (July): 251-261.

Jones-Correa, Michael. 2005. Bringing outsiders in: Questions of immigrant incorporation. In *The politics of democratic inclusion*, ed. Christina Wolbrecht and Rodney E. Hero, 75-101. Philadelphia: Temple University Press.

Kaiser Commission on Medicaid and the Uninsured. 2008. States moving toward comprehensive health care reform. Online resource:
http://www.kff.org/uninsured/kcmu_statehealthreform.cfm.

-----. 2009. Children's health insurance program reauthorizations act of 2009 (CHIRPA). (February) Online resource: http://www.kff.org/medicaid/upload/7863.pdf

Kaushal, Neeraj, Cordelia W. Reimers and David M. Reimers. 2007. Immigrants and the economy. In *The new Americans: A guide to immigration since 1965*. ed. Mary C. Waters and Reed Ueda with Helen B. Marrow, 176-188. Cambridge: Harvard University Press.

Kingdon, John W. 1995. *Agendas, alternatives, and public policies*. 2nd ed. New York: Longman.

Koerin, Beverly. 2003. The settlement house tradition: Current trends and future concerns. *Journal of Sociology and Social Welfare*. 30(2) (June): 53-68.

Ku, Leighton, and Demetrios G. Papademetriou. 2007. Access to health care and health insurance: Immigrants and immigration reform. *Securing the future: US immigrant integration policy, a reader*, ed. Michael Fix, 83-106. Washington, DC: The Migration Policy Institute.

Lawrence, Paul R., and Jay W. Lorsch. 1967. *Organization and environment: Managing differentiation and integration.* Cambridge: Harvard University Press.

LeCompte, Margaret. 1995. Some notes on power, agenda, and voice: A researcher's personal evolution toward critical collaborative research." In *Critical Theory and Educational Research*, ed. Peter L. McLaren and James M. Giarelli, 91-112. Albany: State University of New York Press.

Lee, Taeku, S. Karthick Ramakrishnan, and Ricardo Ramírez. 2006. Transforming politics, transforming America: the political and civic incorporation of immigrants in the United States. Charlottesville: University of Virginia Press.

Levi, Margaret and Gillian Murphy. 2006. "Coalitions of contention: The case of the WTO protests in Seattle." *Political Studies*. 54 (December): 651-70.

Lofland, John and Lyn H. Lofland. 1995. *Analyzing social settings: A guide to qualitative observation and* analysis. 3rd ed. Belmont, CA: Wadsworth Publishing Company.

Logan, John R. 2007. Settlement patterns in metropolitan America. In *The new Americans: A guide to immigration since 1965*. ed. Mary C. Waters and Reed Ueda with Helen B. Marrow, 83-97. Cambridge: Harvard University Press.

Long, Sharon K., Allison Cook, and Karen Stockley. 2009. Health insurance coverage in Massachusetts: Estimates from the 2008 Massachusetts health insurance survey. (March). Washington D.C.: The Urban Institute.
http://www.urban.org/url.cfm?ID=411815

Maxwell, Joseph A. 2005. *Qualitative research design: An interactive approach*. 2nd ed. Thousand Oaks, CA: Sage Publications.

McAdam, Doug, John D. McCarthy, and Mayer N. Zald, eds. 1996. *Comparative perspectives on social movements: Political opportunities, mobilizing structures, and cultural framings.* Cambridge: Cambridge University Press.

McGarvey, Craig. 2004. *Pursuing democracy's promise: Newcomer civic participation in America.* Sebastopol, CA: Grantmakers Concerned with Immigrants and Refugees.

McClain, Paula D., ed. 1993. *Minority group influence: Agenda setting, formulation, and public policy.* Westport: Greenwood Press.

Menjivar, Ceclia. 2000. *Fragmented ties: Salvadoran immigrant networks in America.* Berkeley: CA: University of California Press.

Milkman, Ruth, ed. 2000. *Organizing immigrants: The challenge for unions in contemporary California.* Ithaca: ILR/Cornell University Press.

Mizrahi, Terry and Beth B. Rosenthal. 2001. Complexities of coalition building: Leaders' successes, strategies, struggles and solutions. *Social Work.* 46(1) (January): 63-78.

Mondros, Jacqueline B. and Scott M. Wilson. *Organizing for power and empowerment.* New York: Columbia University Press.

Naples, Nancy A. 1997. A feminist revisiting of the insider/outsider debate: The "outsider phenomenon" in rural Iowa. In *Reflexivity and voice.* ed. Rosanna Hertz, 70-94. Thousand Oaks: Sage Publications.

Nohria, Nitin and Robert Eccles. 1992. *Networks in organizations.* 2nd Ed. Boston: Harvard Business Press.

Oliver, Christine. 1990. Determinants of interorganizational relationships: Integration and future directions. *The Academy of Management Review.* (15)2: 241-265.

Pardo, Mary. 1998. *Mexican american women activists: Identity and resistance in two Los Angeles communities.* Philadelphia: Temple University Press.

Passel, Jeffrey S. 2005. Report: Estimates of the size and characteristics of the undocumented population. March 21. Washington, D.C.: Pew Hispanic Center. http://pewhispanic.org/files/reports/44.pdf.

-----, and D'Vera Cohn. 2009. A portrait of unauthorized immigrants in the United States. April. Washington, D.C.: Pew Hispanic Center. http://pewhispanic.org/files/reports/107.pdf.

Peterson, Erik. 2004. Coming together: Promises and pitfalls of Minnesota's corporate accountability campaigns. In *Partnering for Change: Unions and Community Groups Build Coalitions for Economic Justice*, ed. David B. Reynolds, 88-110. Armonk, NY: M.E. Sharpe.

Petsod, Daranee, Ted Wang, and Craig McGarvey. 2006. Investing in our communities: Strategies for immigrant integration. *GCIR Toolkit*. Sebastopol: Grantmakers Concerned with Immigrants and Refugees.

Però, Davide and John Solomos. 2010. Introduction: Migrant politics and mobilization: Exclusion, engagements, incorporation. *Ethnic and Racial Studies*. 33(1): 1-18.

Portes, Alejandro, Cristina Escobar, and Renelinda Arana. 2008. Bridging the gap: Transnational and ethnic organizations in the political incorporation of immigrants in the United States. *Ethnic and Racial Studies*, 31(6): 1056-1090.

Portes, Alejandro and Rubén Rumbaut. 2001. *Legacies: The story of the immigrant second generation*. Berkeley: University of California Press.

-----. 2006. *Immigrant America: A portrait*. 3nd ed. Berkeley, CA: University of California Press.

Portes, Alejandro and Min Zhou. 1993. The new second generation: Segmented assimilation and its variants. *The ANNALS of the American Academy of Political and Social Science*. 530(1): 74-96.

Powell Walter. 1990. Neither markets nor hierarchies: Network forms of organization. In *Research in Organizational Behavior*, ed. Barry M. Staw and L.L. Cummings, 12: 295– 336. Greenwich, CT: JAI Press.

Putnam, Robert D. 2001. *Bowling alone: The collapse and revival of American community*. New York: Simon and Schuster.

Okie, Susan. 2007. Immigrants and health care—At the intersection of two broken systems. *The New England Journal of Medicine.* 357(6) (August 9): 525-529.

Ragin, Charles C. 1994. *Constructing social research: The unity and diversity of method.* Thousand Oaks, CA: Pine Forge Press.

Rakich, Jonathon S. and Marvin D. Feit. 2001. A life cycle model of public policy issues in health care: The importance of strategic issues management. *Journal of Health & Social Policy.* 13(4): 17-32.

Ramakrishnan, S. Karthick. 2005. *Democracy in immigrant America: Changing demographics and political participation.* Stanford: Stanford University Press.

Ramakrishnan, S. Karthick and Irene Bloemraad, ed. 2008. Introduction: Civic and Political Inequalities. In *Civic hopes and political realities: Immigrants, community organizations, and political engagement,* 1-42. New York: Russell Sage Foundation.

-----. and Celia Viramontes. 2006. *Civic inequalities: Immigrant volunteerism and community organizations in California.* San Francisco: Public Policy Institute of California.

-----. and Thomas J. Espenshade. 2001. Immigrant incorporation and political participation in the United States. *International Migration Review.* 35(3): 870–909.

Reardon-Anderson, Jane, Randolph Capps, Michael E. Fix. 2002. The health and well-being of children in immigrant families. *New Federalism: National Survey of America's Families.* B-52 (November 26). Washington D.C.: The Urban Institute. http://www.urban.org/url.cfm?ID=310584

Reinharz, Shulamit. 1992. *Feminist methods in social research.* New York: Oxford University Press.

-----. 1997. Who am I? The need for a variety of selves in the field. In *Reflexivity and voice.* ed. Rosanna Hertz, 3-20, Thousand Oaks: Sage Publications.

Reyes, Belinda I. 2001. *A portrait of race and ethnicity in California: An assessment of social and economic well-being.* San Francisco: Public Policy Institute of California.

Reynolds, David B, ed. 2004. *Partnering for change: Unions and community groups build coalitions for economic justice*. Armonk, NY: M.E. Sharpe.

Roberts-Degennaro, Maria, and Mizrahi, Terry. 2005. Coalitions as social change agents. In *The handbook of community practice*. ed. Marie Weil, 305-318. Thousand Oaks: Sage Publications, Inc.

Rogers, Mary Beth. 1990. *Cold anger: A story of faith and power politics*. Denton, TX: University of North Texas Press.

Rose, Fred. 2004. Labor-environmental coalitions. In *Partnering for change: Unions and Community Groups Build Coalitions for Economic Justice*, ed. David B. Reynolds, 3-18. Armonk, NY: M.E. Sharpe.

Sabatier, Paul A., ed. 2007. *Theories of the policy process*. 2nd ed. Boulder: Westview Press.

Sabatier, Paul A. and Hank C. Jenkins-Smith. Eds. 1993. *Policy change and learning: An advocacy coalition approach*. Boulder: Westview Press.

Schlozman, Kay Lehman, Sidney Verba and Henry E. Brady. 1999. Civic participation and the equality problem. In *Civic engagement in American democracy*. ed. Theda Skocpol and Morris P. Fiorina. 427-459. Washington, D.C.: Brookings Institution Press.

Schmid-Thomas, Francesca. 1993. Mobilization in crisis: Setting an agenda for minority health through socially transformative action. In *Minority group influence: Agenda setting, formulation, and public policy*, ed. Paula McClain, 169-186. Westport, CT: Greenwood Press.

Schmidley, Dianne A. 2001. Profile of the foreign-born population in the United States: 2000. *US Bureau of the Census Current Population Reports*. P23-206. Washington, DC: US Government Printing Office.

Scott, Richard W. and Gerald F. Davis. 2007. *Organizations and organizing: Rational, natural and open system perspectives*. Upper Saddle River, NJ: Pearson/Prentice Hall.

Sharfman, Mark P., Barbara Gray, and Aimin Yan. 1991. The context of interorganizational collaboration in the garment industry: An institutional perspective." *The Journal of Applied Behavioral Science*, 27(2): 181-208.

Shirley, Dennis. 1997. *Community organizing for urban school reform*. Austin: University of Texas.

Siggelkow, Nicolaj. 2007. Persuasion with case studies. *Academy of Management Journal*. 50(1) (February): 20-24.

Singer, Audrey. 2008. Introduction. In *Twenty-first-century gateways: Immigrant incorporation in suburban America*. ed. Audrey Singer, Susan W. Hardwick, and Caroline B. Brettell. Washington, D.C.: Brookings Institution Press.

Singer, Audrey. 2004. The rise of new immigrant gateways. *The Living Cities Census Series*. Washington D.C.: The Brookings Institution. http://www.ciaonet.org/wps/sia03/sia03.pdf

Sirianni, Carmen. 2009. Investing in democracy: Engaging citizens in collaborative governance. Brookings Institution Press: Washington, D.C.

-----, and Friedland, Lewis. 2001. *Civic innovation in America: Community empowerment, public policy, and the movement for civic renewal*. Berkeley, CA: University of California Press.

Skerry, Peter. 1993. *Mexican Americans: The ambivalent minority*. Cambridge: Harvard University Press.

Skocpol, Theda. 1999. Advocates without members: The recent transformation of American civic life." In *Civic engagement in American democracy*, ed. Theda Skocpol and Morris P. Fiorina, 461-509. Washington, D.C.: The Brookings Institution Press.

-----. 2003. *Diminished democracy: From membership to management in American civic life*. Norman, OK: University of Oklahoma Press.

-----, and Morris P. Fiorina, eds. 1999. *Civic engagement in American democracy*. Washington, D.C.: Brookings Institution Press.

Soyer, Daniel. 2006. Mutual aid societies and fraternal orders. In *A companion to American immigration*, ed. Reed Ueda, 528-546. Malden, MA: Blackwell Publishing.

Sterne, Evelyn Savidge. 2001. Beyond the boss: Immigration and American political culture from 1880 to 1940. In *E pluribus unum?: Contemporary and historical perspectives on immigrant political incorporation*, ed. Gary Gerstle and John Mollenkopf, 33-66. New York: Russell Sage Foundation.

Stevens, Gregory D., Michael R. Cousineau, and Kyoko Rice. 2006. Monitoring the expansion of children's health initiatives in California. *Evaluation highlights: Cover California's kids.* (Keck School of Medicine, University of Southern California). (May). Los Angeles: The California Endowment.

Stone, Clarence N. 1989. *Regime politics: Governing Atlanta, 1946-1988.* Lawrence, KS: University Press of Kansas.

Suárez-Orozco, Carola, and Marcelo M. Suárez-Orozco. 2001. *Children of immigration.* Cambridge: Harvard University Press.

-----. 2007. Education. In *The new Americans: A guide to immigration since 1965.* ed. Mary C. Waters and Reed Ueda with Helen B. Marrow, 243-257. Cambridge: Harvard University Press.

Tarrow, Sidney. 1998. *Power in movement: Social movements and contentious politics.* 2nd Ed. Cambridge: Cambridge University Press.

Tattersall, Amanda, and David Reynolds. 2007. The shifting power of labor-community coalitions: Identifying common elements of powerful coalitions in Australia and the U.S. *WorkingUSA.* 10(1): 77–102.

Taylor, Marilyn. 2003. *Public policy in the community.* New York: Palgrave Macmillan.

Thompson, James D. 2003. *Organizations in action: Social science bases of administrative theory.* New York: McGraw Hill Book Co.

Tichenor, Daniel. 2002. *Dividing lines: The politics of immigration control in America.* Princeton: Princeton University Press.

Trenholm, Christopher, Embry Howell, Ian Hill, and Dana Hughes. 2007. Three independent evaluations of healthy kids programs find dramatic gains in well-being of children and families. *In Brief.* No. 1. (November).

http://www.mathematica-
mpr.com/publications/PDFs/CHIthreeindep.pdf.

Verba, Sidney, Kay Lehman Schlozman, and Henry E. Brady.
1995. *Voice and equality: Civic voluntarism in American politics.*
Cambridge: Harvard University Press.

Viramontes, Celia. 2008. Civic engagement across borders:
Mexicans in southern California. In *Civic hopes and political
realities: Immigrants, community organizations, and political
engagement,* ed. S. Karthick Ramakrishnan and Irene
Bloemraad, 351-381. New York: Russell Sage Foundation.

Waddock, Sandra A. and James E. Post. 1995. Catalytic alliances
for social problem solving. *Human Relations.* 48(8): 951-973.

Wang, Ted, and Robert C. Winn. July 2006. Groundswell meets
groundwork: Recommendations for building immigrant
mobilizations. A Special Report from the Four Freedoms
Fund and Grantmakers Concerned with Immigrants and
Refugees.
http://www.gcir.org/system/files/Groundswell_ReportRE
Vweb.pdf

Warren, Mark E. 2001. *Dry bones rattling: Community building to
revitalize American democracy.* Princeton: Princeton University
Press.

Wcislo, et al. 2007. "Lessons Learned to Date from the
Massachusetts HealthCare Reform." Internal document
prepared for 1199 SEIU United Healthcare Workers East.

Weick, Karl E. 1976. Educational organizations as loosely
coupled system. *Administrative Science Quarterly,* 21(1)
(March): 1-19.

Wolbrecht. Christina. 2005. Mediating institutions. In *The
politics of democratic inclusion,* ed. Christina Wolbrecht and
Rodney E. Hero, 103-107. Philadelphia: Temple University
Press.

Wong, Janelle. 2006. *Democracy's promise: Immigrants and
American civic institutions.* Ann Arbor: University of
Michigan Press.

Wood, Richard L. 2002. *Faith in action: Religion, race, and democratic organizing in America*. Chicago: The University of Chicago Press.

Yin, Robert K. 2003. *Case study research: Design and methods*. 3rd ed. Thousand Oaks, CA: Sage Publications.

Zakocs, Ronda C. and Erika M. Edwards. 2006. What explains community coalition effectiveness? A review of the literature. *American Journal of Preventive Medicine*, 30(4): 351-361.

Zhou, Min. 1997. Segmented assimilation: Issues, controversies, and recent research on the new second generation. *International Migration Review*. Special Issue: Immigrant Adaptation and Native-Born Responses in the Making of Americans 31(4)(Winter): 975-1008.

Index